INSIDE JOB

BOOKS BY TOM WAYMAN

Waiting for Wayman
Free Time
Money and Rain: Tom Wayman Live
For and Against the Moon
Living on the Ground: Tom Wayman Country
A Planet Mostly Sea
The Nobel Prize Acceptance Speech
Beaton Abbott's Got the Contract (ed.)
A Government Job at Last (ed.)
Going for Coffee (ed.)

INSIDE JOB

Essays on the New Work Writing

TOM WAYMAN

Harbour Publishing
1983

Printed and bound in Canada

ISBN: 0-920080-46-4

The cover painting is *Tea Break, Sparwood* by Bill Featherston, reproduced with the permission of B.C. Coal and the artist.

This book was published with the assistance of the Canada Council and the B.C. Cultural Fund.

Harbour Publishing
P.O. Box 219
Madeira Park, B.C.
V0N 2H0

Acknowledgements

The contemporary work literature was anticipated by the Canadian poets Leo Kennedy and Dorothy Livesay writing in the magazine *New Frontier* in the 1930s. In the first issue, June 1936, Kennedy in an essay speaks favorably of "industrial poems" and argues: "We need poetry that reflects the lives of our people, working, loving, fighting, groping for clarity". (from Peter Stevens, ed., *The McGill Movement: A.J.M. Smith, F.R. Scott and Leo Kennedy* [Toronto: Ryerson, 1969]). Livesay, in a later article discussing literature in Canada, states: "It is my theory...that until we look to the people, and the industries, and the economics of our social set-up, we will have no original contribution to make". Concerning Canadian writers, she says: "Their experience is almost wholly confined to one aspect of life, the consumer's. Well and good; that should not prevent good writing. When however the writer, 'the scientist of society' as Zola called him, can see only one half of the stage: when he has no understanding of the life of the producing groups, then surely his picture of what he does know will be lop-sided and untrue?" And Livesay looks forward to the time when "those in the producing categories will speak out for themselves", when "those who have worked in the mills and mines find voice". (Livesay, *Right Hand Left Hand* [Erin, Ont.: Press Porcepic, 1977]).

The present collection of essays is the result of the author's interactions with a great many people. These individuals agreed and disagreed with the ideas here, felt the concepts were too simple or too complex, were clearly stated or confusing: in short, these people offered the usual responses a writer needs to receive from his friends. I am particularly thankful to Perry L. Millar, who heard these ideas batted around innumerable times, who provided inspiration and debate, and who thus assisted these essays to grow from random observations and offhand comments into written form. This book is gratefully dedicated to her. And among those who were especially helpful to the process that produced this collection are: Morris Wayman, Mark Warrior, Jars Balan, Myrna Kostash, Chris Bullock, Artem Lozynsky, Bronwen Wallace, Ron Baxter, Rick Salutin, Jim Daniels, P.J. Laska, Emanuel Fried, Robert Carson, Pat Aufderheidi. Naturally, none of them necessarily approves of all or any of what is said here.

"The Limits of Realism" has been slightly revised since its first publication in *This Magazine* (Toronto) May-June 1977 issue. The essay was subsequently reprinted in Brian Fawcett's *NMFG* (Vancouver) October 1977. An earlier version of Part I of "Regional Culture, National Culture, Industrial Culture" appeared in *This Magazine* February-March 1981 under the title of "Unrealism and Regional Poetry". A shortened version of Part II of "Regional Culture, etc." was published in *Event* (Surrey, B.C.) Spring 1982, entitled "Our Culture, Our Country". The complete essay also appears in *Praxis* (UCLA). "Ground Work" is in the Spring 1983 issue of *Labour/Le Travailleur* (Memorial University) with the title "Inside Job: The Transformation of Literature."

Contents

Introduction: GROUND WORK

I became interested in writing about daily work because of a moment in my own past. When I attended the University of British Columbia in the mid-1960s, those of us who were studying creative writing were expected to give a graduating recital of our literary efforts. As I looked through my material to prepare for this, I realized that the subjects of my poems were entirely different than the concerns of my ordinary waking hours. This was a revelation. I had assumed until then that the poems which I had spent many hours creating and nurturing would, when viewed together, represent an accurate depiction of my life. After all, this was why I wanted to be a writer: to share with other people what I noticed about the condition of being alive.

Since I had failed in my poems to live up to my aim, I vowed that at least a majority of any future writing would concern itself with what I found most important about my daily existence. Thus, when I finished school and began to work, I wrote some poems about the people and conditions I met at the various blue-collar and white-collar jobs I held.

In the early 1970s it became important for me to compare my poems about work with those by other people. In my formal studies of writing I had learned the benefits of a careful reading of other authors who had grappled with and solved certain artistic problems I might be having—problems such as getting another voice to "speak" in a poem, or strategies for ending a poem, and so on. I had a vague sense that the portrayal of work in poetry was a subject all to itself and I began to search for contemporary poems by others about working.

Eventually I gathered a file of these, and in 1974 NeWest Press of Edmonton published the first small anthology of work poems I assembled, *Beaton Abbot's Got the Contract.* The title comes from a poem by a Newfoundland high school student about his hope of driving truck for a living after graduation.

Once *Beaton Abbot's Got The Contract* appeared, friends and acquaintances began to locate more poems about contemporary work and point them out to me. These poems are found throughout the usual literary life of our times—in volumes by individual authors, literary periodicals and anthologies. Because people were aware of my interest in the topic, they would show me unpublished material by themselves or people they knew, as well. I quickly had enough work poems for a second, larger anthology, which MacLeod Books in Vancouver published in 1976. It was called *A Government Job At Last*, the title phrase taken from a poem by a Mountie about his occupation.

By this time I was living in Windsor, Ontario, where I met Artem Lozynsky. Lozynsky had graduated with a PhD in English from Wayne State University in Detroit, and out of an interest in the French mystic Simone Weil's writings about her employment Lozynsky read much of *A Government Job At Last* in manuscript. Lozynsky was the first person who saw the work poems as worthy of critical study. I had already concluded that the *Beaton Abbot* collection was not entirely satisfying because it contains poems about contemporary work both as seen from the outside (someone watching somebody else work) and as seen from the inside (someone writing about a job they have done themselves or otherwise know intimately). I had decided to limit *A Government Job* and any subsequent anthologies to work poems written from the *insider's* perspective, as these to me are the most accurate, honest and successful. But Lozynsky had thought further about what the contemporary work poems considered as a whole might demonstrate. I found his ability to look beyond the surface of these poems to be extremely stimulating. In many ways the essays contained in the present volume, *Inside Job,* owe their origin to his conviction that there is more to the new industrial literature than a cursory glance might indicate.

Inside Job gathers together the essays I have written and published since 1976 concerning the poetry, fiction and drama written by participants in the contemporary North American work world about their experiences on the job. These essays offer an overview of my conclusions about the significance of this writing. They do not intend a line-by-line or motif-by-motif analysis of individual authors or literary works. Instead, they discuss what I feel the appearance of this writing suggests about our literature's past, present and potential.

In brief, "The Limits of Realism" considers the dominant mode of the new industrial writing—realism. It looks at some reasons why realism can be considered high art in the visual arts but low art when found in literature. "The Limits of Realism" examines the differences between the old External Realism (including socialist realism) and the new Internal Realism (as evidenced in contemporary work poetry).

"Regional Culture, National Culture, Industrial Culture" assesses in whose interests the fine arts culture of a region or the nation presently functions. Then the piece explores the cultural world a majority of Canadians inhabit, using "cultural" now in its broader definition. The essay argues that much of our lives are spent in an industrial culture generated by the current methods of organizing the production of society's goods and services. And that very little of our literature comes out of or is addressed to the culture in which a majority of us live. The new industrial literature is seen as the first consciously artistic productions of the contemporary industrial culture.

"The Enemies of Intelligence" considers two groups— the authoritarian left, and literary scholars and teachers— who have been resistant to a wider acceptance of the new writing as central to an understanding of our society. The response of these people demonstrates a reluctance on their part to examine the specific criticisms of contemporary society contained in the industrial literature. Such a lack of critical thinking about daily work represents an opposition by these groups to intelligence and creativity in everyday life.

Finally, *Inside Job* closes with a selected bibliography of recent work writing.

Some of the loudest objections to the ideas implied by the emergence of the new work literature have come from other authors. It is as though these people sense that the appearance of the new writing indicates a major change in attitude to literature as we have known it. Traditionally, the three main subjects of imaginative writing in English have been love, death and nature. To these, the contemporary industrial literature introduces a fourth major subject: work. More than this, the new writing about the job demonstrates how a person's attitudes to love, death and nature are in large part shaped by the kind of daily work he or she does. Our employment obviously determines our personal standard of living—how well and where we live off the job. Our employment is responsible, too, for how much mental and physical energy we have when we return home, and indeed how much time off we receive. So the amount of money, energy and time available to us to pursue romance or appreciate nature is a direct result of the conditions of our work. And how we regard and respond to a wide range of matters, including death and nature and the opposite sex, is strongly influenced by whether we interact with these daily at the job and what this interaction or lack of interaction leads us to conclude about them. Any literature, then, which omits this governing experience of daily life is a literature with an enormous hole in the middle of it. Just as a taboo once surrounded the presentation of sex in literature, so a detailed examination of daily work and its effects on people has up to the present been omitted from most of our imaginative writing.

The response of some writers to these observations is to claim that these concepts must lead to authors being *told* what they have to write. I don't believe this is true. The emerging women's movement, for example, showed that in much of what is published women appear in negative, passive and restricted roles. Subsequently, feminist critics have been able to point to and discuss sexism in literature, whether such sexism is blatantly or implicitly portrayed in a literary work. But such criticism has not stopped authors from writing whatever they want. If a writer chooses to be sexist, he or she is free to do so. Yet the women's movement reserves the right to continue to identify sexism in literature wherever it appears and to demonstrate the harmful effects on human beings such sexism has.

I feel exactly the same standards apply to a discussion of the absence of daily work in our literature to date. While writing is a solitary and personal act, writing for publication is a social act. A published poem, play or story appears in a particular society at a specific time. And whether or not the author likes to think about it, the published work has certain effects in that society.

Today most of our cultural productions—and I refer here to the fine art and popular culture of books, paintings, music, television, movies—have the effect of leading people away from the affairs of our everyday life into another world. Put charitably, most good writing can enable people to forget their own troubles for a little while.

Looked at another way, though, this writing is part of a larger culture industry that, in all its branches, does not encourage us to examine our daily lives, to understand the sources of our problems, and to act individually or collectively to improve our existence. The negative term for these products of our culture industry is that they are escapist. And as long as our literature overwhelmingly leads us into the bondage of beautiful dreams, or into following the imaginary problems of impossible people, our inevitable return to daily reality will be a disappointment.

Much of our cultural world at present, then, functions as a narcotic. It numbs people so they can withdraw for a short time into the illusion of an impossible but apparently-more-interesting world. This is where money, success and fame are to be found now in the field of culture.

Yet I believe there is another role for the writer than that of narcotics pedlar. Writers might ask *why* there is such a demand for escape from everyday life in our society—escape through drugs, TV, alcohol or attending most literary and other cultural events. What is the failure at the core of our daily lives that leads so many of us to seek solace in another, illusory place?

For the flaw in cultural escapism is that the escapist *doesn't* escape. What we term escape literature is actually status quo literature. It in no way leads to any change in the conditions of our daily existence that led us to want to escape. Hence, the reader immediately needs another fix. That is why people who defend this direction in modern culture on the grounds that "it gives people what they want" are wrong. What people appear to want desperately, in enormous numbers, is to *live* in a space that is better than this one. And this they don't get from their hit of culture.

I believe school is where we learn to regard literature as though it is insulated from the everyday. In a typical high school English class, the students may be worried about family breakdown, drugs, sex, careers, and so on. But at the front of the classroom, an English teacher is earnestly insisting that Hamlet's or Macbeth's problems are universal, and so very relevant now. And therefore the class should pay attention to them, especially if the students want to pass.

The irrelevancy of most *contemporary* imaginative writing we are introduced to in high school affects our attitude toward literature as well. This writing also mostly asks readers to put aside their pressing personal and social concerns and go chasing after the writer's rainbows. And by directing readers away from any familiar context, how can such writing let the reader judge for himself or herself the veracity of anything the author is saying?

Thus we learn to regard good literature more or less as science fiction. It is an interesting or boring diversion about unlikely solutions to imaginary difficulties that are literally light-years away from our own daily lives. Put another way, we learn that serious literature consists of overwritten escape books.

There is a social consequence of this with which I feel writers should be deeply concerned. The majority of people who continue to read after high school flock directly to romantic fiction, escape literature of the most obvious kind. For if someone has learned that reading is a means to try to escape from daily life, why shouldn't he or she choose a book in which escape is more simply presented than in the "artistic" brand of escape literature appreciated mainly by a small number of intellectuals and their graduate students? And thus most serious collections of new poems and fiction are lucky to sell a few thousand copies.

Nevertheless, in my experience many writers resent any exploration of the effects their writing has on other human beings. These authors prefer discussions of their work's form, or use of images, and so on. Any social consequences of their art are not part of the usual critical vocabulary, either.

Not that the social effect of a literary work should be the only subject for consideration in evaluating writing. But even the currently-accepted critical standards for examining literature can be scrutinized from this point of view. For example, magic realism as derived from Garcia Marquez' *One Hundred Years of Solitude* is held by many critics to be an exciting development in contemporary English-language fiction. But if magic realism in practice is defined as a bizarre and arbitrary surrealism, we might ask why this technique now enjoys such critical approval. Is it because magic realism eases the reader's flight into fantasy, especially a reader jaded with imaginative writing which employs more conventional narrative and descriptive techniques in its attempt to remove the reader temporarily from ordinary life?

Similarly, if serious literature is intended to be a diversion for a social elite, as some will argue as a defense of the present literary situation, then the rest of us still have the right to examine the literary standards such writing is supposed to uphold. We would not be surprised to discover that these standards implicitly support the concept of social hierarchies. For instance, critics will refer to an author's familiarity with Greek or other ancient myths (once held by the elite to be a sign of a truly educated person) as an illustration of that author's literary skill. Yet a case can be made that an understanding of such mythology has nothing to do with literary accomplishment. Rather, offering praise for the appearance of these myths in a literary work, at a time when knowledge of such myth has virtually disappeared from public awareness, simply maintains an elitist attitude toward education and imaginative writing.

Well-written escape literature is at times defended

critically on the grounds it provides a vision of other human possibilities, often of an ideal world or situation. But every ideal has an historical basis. To a person who today is hungry, the ideal world to aspire to is one in which everyone is fed. So we can scrutinize the basis of the ideal presented in imaginative writing. If, for instance, the literary piece in question ignores the influence that daily work has on our lives, then the vision this writing presents merely restates what most of our literature already conveys: that goods and services are somehow not produced by people living in societies organized around such production. Thus the fantasy the reader is offered is thoroughly disconnected from any possibility of attainment. Far from postulating a vision worth striving for, then, this literature offers attempted escape of the usual, impossible type. The harm it does is that, because of the prevailing taboo, once again we are blocked from any consideration of the largest influence on our daily existence. And this includes consideration of what the ideal forms of production of our necessary goods and services might be.

The women's movement has already demonstrated the social effects of writing which ignores current realities under the guise of sketching a supposedly better alternative. For example feminist critics have detailed what occurs when, against all known realities, such literature posits marriage as the ideal state or as the culminating vision of happiness for women. Where such writing is particularly effective, and hence believed, expectations are raised which experience shows result in very painful episodes for people when these expectations are revealed to be false and unattainable. In the same way, a vision meant to inspire human beings which does not take into account the effects on them of what they must do all day to survive and/or prosper is not of much use except as a misleading and potentially hurtful dream.

Experimental writing, too, often seems remote from an

exploration of the central issues of our daily lives. Yet we know from science that experiments must go on if the boundaries of what we know, of what we can do, are to be pushed back. And we also know from science that a great many experiments fail. But we can learn as much or more from a failed experiment as we can from a successful one.

Experimental writing has its own social consequences, however. Formal experimentation (that is, experiments involving artistic *form*) has increased during the past three-quarters of a century to become what many artists now practicing think art is supposed to be about. Formal experimentation, be it "new music" or "abstract expressionism", is art about art. And that means an end of a critique of society in art.

Why should the absence of this critique matter? It matters because the literary arts today are one of the last potentially free spaces in modern industrial society. Journalism and entertainment writing are closely controlled by, or in the interests of, the business corporations. These are organizations whose primary goal is not to improve the life of the human race, but to make money. It is in the interests of these corporations, and with their encouragement, that the arts are directed to be self-obsessed. Not *what* is said or thought is to be debated, but instead *how* it is expressed. Don't ask if the knife can cut, but consider its shape, its formal novelties, its weight, its surface texture. With the blocking of art as a critique of society, the circle of control is virtually complete. Who is left to question how daily life is organized, or the wisdom of the self-appointed managers of our destiny? When voices of protest or opposition do arise, who is skilled enough at critical thinking to prevent these voices from being co-opted, perverted, led back into the paths the corporations choose for them to go?

The moment an author puts pen to paper is the same significant instant experienced by everyone in this society who works. Our contemporary society continues in its present form not because a collection of "elected representatives" sits at city hall or in a building in the national capital. Society continues in its accustomed patterns because through our work each day we reproduce all the component parts and relationships that were in effect yesterday. There can be no meaningful social change until in our daily working lives we rebuild the world into freer, less exploitative patterns than we did formerly.

Any human-made object in the world—including a typewriter or electronic word processor—contains a past, present and various possible futures. The past is concerned with the human lives that went into gathering all the components of the object, and with the lives that were involved in the conception and production of the object itself. In the present, now, that object—whether a hammer to be used in the construction of a house, or the lever of a drill press—is held poised by someone who is going to put it to use. As the object is held, alternative futures are grasped too. Will the object be used as it has been in daily life up to now? Or, will the object be used in a new way: will it be part of a rebuilding of daily life in a different, preferably more humane and democratic manner? The brain functions, the hand moves, and the world is created again from this tiniest and most significant of actions.

So with a writer, good or bad. As the pen touches paper, the writer can either help keep the world going in its old oppressive patterns, or begin through what he or she writes to help bring about a better world. Naturally, words by themselves will not create any improvement in our common lives. Yet by demystifying and making clearer the past, by bringing forth what is hidden in our present society, and by suggesting other potential futures than those the people over us in society's hierarchies have planned for us, an author can take part in the construction of a happier planet. But this starts for a writer each day at the tip of the pen he or she lifts. Will he or she refuse to produce more of what deludes and deceives, however prettily or fashionably done?

What we need, I feel, is imaginative writing which seeks to fearlessly examine the current state of affairs, and which aims to assist us in discovering solutions to our urgent social and personal problems. To me, the new industrial writing is the beginning of such a literature. Another recent manifestation was the first upsurge of feminist writing. This broke away from the literary and cultural traditions of depicting women, and spoke directly about the contemporary situation of half the human race and about the need for major change to improve the situation. But such writing is not the mainstream of our culture. That mainstream, when it does deal with everyday existence, continues to present contemporary lives as trivialized, romanticized or mythologized beyond belief.

Meanwhile, a further response by some authors to the new industrial literature concerns the question: isn't literary composition work? Writers know they often put in long hours at their desks, and so they ask why, say, a poem about the act of writing isn't a work poem. Of course there is a sense in which such a poem is, but in my anthologies of contemporary work poetry I have not included these. For one thing, there is nothing new about this kind of writing; authors have described and used as a metaphor the act of literary composition for a long time. There even already exist anthologies of poems about poetry. More importantly, though, the conditions under which authors create are vastly different than the conditions under which contemporary wage labor occurs. Most creative writers can set their own hours; most do not feel the constant pressure of direction from a supervisor; all can leave the place of work on a whim; most do not depend on their creative work for their economic survival; and so on. In short, this is work that writers have *chosen* to do under conditions they ordinarily establish *themselves.*

Some authors will protest that they "work hard" when they write, and of couse they do. But the question is surely *what* does someone work hard at? Strenuous effort in a pointless or destructive cause obviously is no virtue. My observation is that many writers duly put in hours and hours at the desk, but don't want to do the hard work necessay to understand the economic and social lives of themselves or their fellow citizens. They prefer to emote and fantasize on paper in the hope that they are thus contributing to culture.

The importance of the new industrial literature, I believe, lies rather in its ability to accurately express the conditions of daily life of a majority of the population. But since that majority traditionally has almost no contact with contemporary imaginative writing, people will sometimes ask how representative of their fellow employees the new work writers are. The questioner will point to the advanced educational level, generally youthful age, and comparatively short period of employment at particular jobs of many of these authors.

But biographical details are not the issue with work writers, any more than they are with any other author. No critic would insist that a war poet, for instance, be a career soldier with many years experience in combat. What is important to us as readers is the effectiveness and accuracy of the literature created by the war writer. Similarly, we don't ask of the writer of a love poem that he or she be widely experienced, and/or remain in love with the specific individual about whom the poem was written, in order for that poem to continue to be regarded as an accurate and moving description of being in love under a certain set of conditions. Rather than consider the biography of the author, we ask ourselves: is the poem convincing to us? And especially: is it convincing based on our own experiences of being in love?

The enthusiastic reception the new work poems have received from those working at the jobs depicted—irrespective of the poet's background, or how long the poet has been employed, or whether the poet still works there—is testimony to the truth and power of these poems, I feel. The only way biography seems to enter into consideration is that personal participation by the poet in the situation described allows the poet to select and portray detail only an *insider* could know. This is detail that helps give the poem authenticity to an audience knowledgeable about the job. Similarly, a veteran will have a different response to a poem written by someone who has evidently been in combat than to a poem written by someone describing war in more general terms, someone who seems to lack detailed knowledge of the actual experiences involved.

Overall, too, authors are seldom typical of the milieu their writings depict. The very act of close observation, with the intent of incorporating what is observed into art, separates a writer or any artist from the people around him or her. These other people also reflect on events. But they usually express the conclusions such reflection leads them to in other ways than by struggling to put words on paper. Margaret Atwood's biography and lifestyle, for example, hardly makes her a "typical" or "representative" woman or Canadian. Yet feminist or nationalist critics find much in her writing that seems to them correct and effective portrayals of women's or Canadian issues.

Because the new industrial literature has been so warmly accepted by those employed with the writers at the jobs—allowing, of course, for the usual variations in response to *any* experience found among any group of human beings—I feel confident in making the claims that I do about this writing. Robert Pring-Mill, in an essay entitled "The Redemption of Reality Through Documentary Poetry", looks at the Nicaraguan poet-priest-politician Ernesto Cardenal's writings and draws conclusions similar to my view of the new industrial literature (from Cardenal's *Zero Hour* [New York: New Directions, 1980]):

> These poems demand more than just an alert response, because the poet wishes to prod us beyond thought and into action: his texts are never just concerned to document and understand reality, but also to help change it.... But the data

> have to be recorded before reality can be reshaped, and the reshaping lies beyond the poems themselves....

This triple concern—to document reality, to do so in order to help alter reality for the better, and to do so in the form of imaginative writing—lies at the heart of what I see happening in the work writing. A younger Canadian poet and critic, John Lent, has already found in the work poems what he considers to be a new literary technique. In his essay, "The Lyric As Documentary" (*Contemporary Verse Two*[Winnipeg] August 1982), Lent contrasts the long documentary poem on various topics with the usually-shorter contemporary work poem:

> In so many of the...poems the objective, sometimes raw facts of work are counterpointed with and transfigured by the subjective view of those facts. The result is the lyrical poem as documentary. The worlds documented are as widely separated as the hilariously detailed universe of the kitchen in a fast-food hamburger joint, or the stainless steel surfaces of a hospital delivery room.

Lent sees this new technique of lyrical documentary as an extension of William Carlos Williams' poetics.

> It is an experiment in which the very raw facts of ordinary life are subjected to the shifting, layered lenses of consciousness and emotion, and then allowed to revolve, suspended in its two fields of concrete and abstract light, shining, as in some of the best poems of William Carlos Williams. It was, after all, an experiment Williams insisted upon and pursued throughout his long career.

But to me, the critical significance of the new work writing is that it constitutes a transformation of literature itself. Historically, the absence of the subject of daily work in literature is probably due to the privileged background and/or position of the majority of writers and readers. But the increased access to post-secondary education since World War II, plus the growing awareness of some professionals that their work world shares aspects in common with many other types of employees, has resulted in the emergence of writers able to depict actual daily work in our society and the effects this work has on the range of human activities and attitudes on and off the job. The contemporary industrial literature thus presents far more accurately than does what has previously been written how most people in our society actually experience reality.

Once the implications of this become evident to a reader, a certain impatience with much contemporary writing develops. Because the central experience of daily life is still almost everywhere missing, the literature which forms the basis of our literary culture appears shallow and hollow. We may look at love stories, adventure tales, surreal and intentionally absurd accounts of individuals in the past, present or future. But in few cases is daily work a concern of the characters whose interaction makes up the events chronicled in this writing.

An appreciation of the centrality of work to most people's existence can also change how we regard the literature of the past. In Shakespeare's plays, for instance, the characters whose actions shape history are the nobility. Ordinary people are clowns, buffoons who don't even speak in verse the way the important figures of Shakespeare's plots do. We know, however, that it was the work of farmers, artisans, housewives, soldiers and other ordinary folk that produced the wealth and power arrangements which allowed the nobility the leisure to squabble with each other over the spoils or to meditate on the meaning of life. So Shakespeare's plays seem propaganda for the point of view which asserts that the wealthy are the significant individuals in a society and those who work for a living are comic and/or prosaic but basically unimportant. This is a similar message to that conveyed by the flood of contemporary books, movies and television productions which insists it is the rich, or at least those people who don't have to work for money each day for a living, whose activities are the most significant in society and hence the most worthy of presentation.

By observing the inclusion or absence of a depiction of daily work and its effects in any imaginative writing—historical or contemporary—we obtain a critical tool which can assist us to sort out what an author is telling us in addition to the obvious content. We might agree, for example, that Shakespeare is a skilful writer, able to bring to life the personalities of rich Elizabethans and to elaborate intricate and absorbing plots. But at the same time we can conclude that his message regarding the position of working people in society is odious.

I believe such an awareness of the subject of work will transform our appreciation of the literature of the past while it transforms the literature produced in the future. Work, though, will not become a major subject because some writer is forced to consider its effects on his or her characters. Rather, like the slow ending of sexist portrayals of women in imaginative writing, the realistic portrayal of daily work will be adopted by authors because it is a vital step forward in the human race's ability to tell a story. As in the depiction of women, we move from a flawed, limited description of human life to a fuller, more accurate one. Most writers I have met, except those irretrievably lost to pandering to the status quo for fame or money, are interested in extending the powers of the written word to depict human existence. So I feel a widespread acceptance of work as a central subject in imaginative writing is inevitable.

Further, I am convinced the new working poems and other industrial literature are part of the first emergence on this planet of a truly adult literature. The imaginative writing we have had up to now has largely been unequal to the task of honestly presenting the experiences of the men and women who constitute a majority of our population. Just as a child or adolescent often does not understand work or money, so our literature mostly has ignored these and focussed instead on the unlikely lives of those whose day-to-day existence apparently is not governed by concerns of work or money: the rich, killers, outlaws, or fantastic representations of people doing certain real jobs (doctors, cowboys, policemen, and so on).

The new work writing takes up the challenge of portraying the world an adult sees and attempts to understand and/or change. A grown person who constantly evades having to cope with reality, who lives in a world of dreams however beautiful, we consider immature if not mentally ill. The contemporary industrial writing provides maturity and a healthy balance to literature.

It is perhaps appropriate that poetry should be at the forefront of this development. To most people, thanks in large part to high school English curriculums, the words "poetic" and "romantic" are considered synonymous. And Romantic poetry as introduced to us in school is an archetype of escape from reality in art. So poetry is widely understood to be that property found in the writings of a small group of mainly upper-class Englishmen who, at the start of the 19th Century, turned their faces away from the horrors of the Industrial Revolution occurring around them and wrote about sweet fantasies, daffodils, nightingales.

But the Romantics at least shook their art free from the sterile and rigid order of the preceeding poetries. And now the new work poetry leads in breaking the remaining shackles of Romanticism in art—obscurity, escape—in order to help us learn more about the everyday world we inhabit. Hence, another way of viewing the new work writing's transformation of literature is that this writing brings to a close the Romantic movement. With the new writing, we end the Romantic conception of the artist as solitary, dreamy, irrational, divinely inspired, extravagant in creating personal images and other artistic puzzles that require a corps of elite critical specialists to decipher and make available for consumption in schools or the market place. In science, as Thomas S. Kuhn has shown (in *The Structure of Scientific Revolutions* [Chicago: University of Chicago Press, 1962]), research repeatedly returns to pivotal historical moments when one course of studies was abandoned in favor of another which subsequently has led to a dead end. When the previously-abandoned line of thought is resumed, breakthroughs in solving certain problems sometimes are made —breakthroughs occasionally major enough to be called scientific revolutions. I believe that in the same way the new work writing takes literature back to the moment when the Romantics recoiled from the beginnings of our industrial civilization. Moving forward from this point, along the path of an honest exploration of our industrial life, literature enters a new era.

Imagine art that presents not just what this person or that claims is hidden in his or her unconscious, but instead depicts what is suppressed in our society. For what is more mysterious, concealed, than the myriad technologies and economic and social relationships, the millions of human lives, that in a complex civilization such as ours are necessary to bring us the simplest of objects we use in our daily life? Also, obscured by widespread acceptance, at the core of daily work is a profoundly undemocratic social structure by means of which production is currently organized. But there is nothing mythological or divine about what is secret here. Just human work, and the lives, loves, deaths, and natural and urban environments that work affects.

As with any new human endeavor, though, the development of industrial literature will not be a triumphal march along a route marked out in advance. As part of the youthful vigor and confusion of any artistic movement in its earliest stages, various debatable issues and possible alternate directions to be followed have already emerged. Some of these questions concern the imaginative writing that has been produced, and some involve the work writers themselves.

For example, to date most of the new work writing has adopted the anecdotal mode: recounting incidents from the working life as experienced by the author or his or her fellow employees. These anecdotes often have been repeated in conversation a number of times before they ever are written down. So when they appear on paper, they have the considerable force of any retold story from which inessential detail has been pruned and where the point or substance has been refined or embellished. But can these anecdotes be used as *images* are now? That is, could a series of related anecdotes be used in a poem, say, in such a manner that their power is further enhanced? This would be parallel to the manner in which images can gain strength and effectiveness in imaginative writing by their placement within the work and their relationship to each other. Also: a good anecdote contains its own message, whether directly or indirectly stated. We see this clearly in the short, sharp work poems that basically consist of one strong anecdote. Similarly, an image needs no commentary; indeed, comment or explanation would detract from the power of an image. But could anecdotal material be used in a longer piece, as images are now, to create general conclusions in the reader's mind about some theme without the direct intervention of the author in the form of commentary?

Another issue arising from the new industrial writing considers an author's use of experience versus imagination. In "The Limits of Realism" I distinguish between the new Internal and older External Realism, praising the contemporary work writers for drawing on their personal, insider's experience of jobs to describe what happens there. Obviously, an enormous amount could be written about a particular plant employing hundreds of men and women. It is even presumably possible for an author to base a great quantity of material on one suitable industrial experience, much as James Joyce took the city of Dublin at a certain period as the setting of story after story, book after book. But we are dealing here with *imaginative* writing. Stephen Crane has related how he interviewed American Civil War veterans, listened closely to their tales of combat, and then added his own responses to participating in organized team sports in order to write *The Red Badge of Courage.* This novel was praised by veterans as an accurate account of battle's effect on Civil War-era soldiers. In a similar manner, it would seem possible for one of the new work writers to combine his or her own experiences as an employee with formal and informal research to create a literary offering dealing with a work situation which appears correct to those employed at that job, even though the author has not personally worked there.

Two examples of matters affecting the work writers themselves are the degree of literary skill they possess and the existence of two distinct types of "worker-writers".

As mentioned above, how skilled an author is considered to be depends on a set of criteria greatly influenced by *who* is doing the assessing. Yet each of us finds some writings more effective than others. By "effective" we can mean anything from "emotionally moving" to "politically correct", factors which can say as much about whoever is making the judgment as they do about the writing itself. We are taught in high school that certain literary works are "good". But the class we are in might almost unanimously find these works boring and irrelevant, and the teacher might be unable to explain what makes this writing "good" other than that it is included in the official curriculum. Nevertheless, we learn to make such assessments of what we read. We want to classify our reading, even if only to identify what we might want to read again or otherwise refer back to. But I feel we must each be aware of the *origins* of our values and inclinations, and thus be able to explain specifically *why* we rank a literary work as we do.

My own belief is that writing is a human skill like talking or making kites or auto repair. I don't think there is such a thing as innate talent, but rather the more one practices a skill the better one becomes at it. By "better" I mean that a broader range of abilities are mastered, an increasing number of problems to do with the activity can be solved, and that the practioner can start to add to humanity's collective knowledge about the skill and not just repeat techniques that have already been discovered. When the skill is the transfer of a repeatedly orally-expressed account (such as a personal experience or anecdote) onto paper, sometimes a person who has no particular facility with writing can be dazzling in what he or she produces. But if this person wishes to tackle a broader range of material, he or she must practice writing skills (which include reading and thinking about other writers' efforts) in order to achieve a sustained high level of literary accomplishment. This is no different than how someone interested in developing carpentry skills has to practice these (including studying building codes and other manuals and observing and assessing the work of other carpenters). Some people may appear to have a "natural" talent for writing, but I believe at some point in their background—at school, at home, or among peers—they were rewarded socially for their use of words. Thus they have since practiced this skill until they have reached their present level of competence in writing.

Obviously some people have or make more opportunity to practice writing than others. Since literature generally comes out of a consideration of one's experiences, and out of time available to set down on paper some results of such consideration, those individuals in society with more leisure time have in the past dominated the production of literature. Among contemporary authors, however, two types of new work writers are currently visible.

One group, which includes most publishing North

American work writers, are people employed at various jobs who write about their work but who are also interested or involved in the ordinary literary life of the age: publishing their writing in literary journals, small press collections, and so on. These authors may be very committed to the concept of work writing, or not. And like all work writers of whatever variety they also write about other topics.

The second group are individuals who for a variety of reasons, from self-expression to participation in adult education programs, have tried their hand at writing about their working lives. Publication or partial self-definition as a writer is not a factor in their interest in writing. This second group is closer to the British model, where the new coalition of groups called the Federation of Worker Writers and Community Publishers emphasizes, besides community creative writing workshops, ventures such as adult basic literacy classes, preparation and publication of literacy texts based on work experiences, preparation and publication of personal and community oral histories, and so on. Participants in this second group, although they are unquestionably also workers who write, more often choose themes for their imaginative writing drawn from the prevailing literary subjects of love, nature and death considered separately from the job and its effects on these and most other aspects of daily life.

The two classifications of work writers are not necessarily static, though. For instance, faced with a literary climate presently not very receptive to imaginative writing about jobs, an aspiring author may give up his or her search for publication and be content with self-expression or sharing his or her writing with friends. Or, a member of the second group of work writers may gain enough self-confidence to seek publication in the more standard literary outlets. In addition, as the work writing movement develops, whatever boundaries that now exist between these two catagories may well disappear.

But however contemporary industrial literature evolves,

the new writing has already started to pull away the veil which so far has cloaked the conditions of our daily work. We pride ourselves on being citizens of a democracy. And yet for the eight hours each day we are employed there is virtually no democracy for us with respect to either management or (in many cases) the union, and precious few rights and privileges. These hours on the job are the ones in which all the nation's goods and services, and hence its wealth and might and standard of living, are created. Yet those of us who are employed have little or no control over the usefulness or uselessness of the product or service we make, nor the uses to which the product may be put, nor the effect our place of work has on the environment. At the job, our participation in decision-making is reduced to the lowest possible level consistent with completion of the tasks assigned to us. And we are paid only a portion of the value of what we produce, according to a highly arbitrary system. Our length of employment, the duration or quality of our education or training, our position in an externally-determined management hierarchy, or how militant the present or former work force in this plant or in this trade has been can determine whether we receive more or less pay than the person working beside us.

Yet the job is the center of our civilization and of our personal lives. So I am convinced work will one day become and be considered a major subject in our literature. When this happens, the work writing movement can be said to have achieved a partial success. If the new industrial literature is ever entirely successful, I feel, daily work will be recognized as *the* central concern in our literature, as in life.

THE LIMITS OF REALISM

My aim here is to consider a question involving that general artistic classification known as realism. What intrigues me is why realism in contemporary painting currently is accepted as high art (i.e., subject to a great deal of critical and academic attention) while the productions of realist poets such as the contemporary work poets is largely treated as low art. Are there limits to realism which account for this situation?

When I refer to realist art, I mean a painting or poem that a viewer or reader believes shows a portion of the world of ordinary reality. Both contemporary figurative painting and writing share a common problem: that the viewer or reader may merely point to the objects he or she recognizes in the work and say, "That's a tree ..." or "That's a logger ..." without having any inclination to probe any deeper, to see the thought or concept that moves the painter or writer to want to set down that tree or that logger before the eye of the mind. Also, it has been suggested to me that modern realist painting even can be considered as suffering from a drawback that doesn't plague realist poetry—a lack of energy. Compare the total calm of a Christopher Pratt seascape with the excitement and motion of an Al Purdy poem, and I think the truth of this assertion is evident. And yet, contemporary realist painting at present is considered high art whereas in the universities to my knowledge the preference in contemporary Canadian literature classes is usually to direct students to examine what to me are silly poems about, say, "the idea of the landscape", rather than the work of our realist poets. I used to believe this was partly due to conditions within the education industry. If students can grasp right away what is happening in a poem, then there is no use for a professor of English to explain the work to them. So the schools concentrate on teaching the difficult, the obscure, the baffling in our literature. However, with realist painting, too, there is an easy surface recognition of objects. But the paintings still merit close examination and discussion, unlike with realist poetry where the apparent assumption is that the surface is all there is.

I have become convinced that the explanation for the current state of affairs does not lie in the limitations of realism itself but rather in the way contemporary art is *perceived.* When I say "perceived" I mean how art is perceived in our society *now,* by human beings living in an historical time. In English-speaking Canada at present, most of that audience for art statistically must be a tiny percentage of the population of Toronto (I base this on publishers' sales figures and the presence there of a majority of the nations's galleries, etc.). We know a little bit, too, about what that audience is like. They are educated, reasonably affluent or (in the case of university students) likely to become so, and they work at jobs that they either find satisfying or else retain the hope that one day they will find jobs that will be satisfying. All these characteristics of course color their perception of art. And, given the way our society is presently structured, the perception of art by these people is pretty well accepted as our society's norm. So, to simplify greatly, it seems to me that for the present the following is:

HOW CONTEMPORARY ART IS PERCEIVED, or WAYMAN'S FOUR-SQUARE GOSPEL OF ART

	Fashionable	**Primary Concern:**
referential	non-referential	Ideas or Techniques **HIGH**
		Events **LOW**

High art, then, is art that people see as having as its *primary* concern a consideration of ideas or techniques. Low art is that which is seen as primarily dealing with events. Both low and high art may be further divided into art which is referential and non-referential. I want to use a common-sense definition for these last two terms: referential art appears to me to be art which fairly evidently refers to real objects and/or occurrences. Someone standing in front of a referential painting can fairly easily recognize objects represented there, and someone reading a referential poem can reasonably readily tell what is happening in the poem.

As well, whether art is high or low, the more non-referential it is the more fashionable it is. There is some art, I think, that despite general agreement that it is high, will never be subject to the amount of discussion, display, or purchase that fashionable art receives. Non-referential art, for whatever historical reasons, appears to be the usual preference of the present audience.

So much for the setting. Let me drop in some examples which I hope will clarify what I mean.

HOW CONTEMPORARY ART IS PERCEIVED

	Fashionable		**Primary Concern:**
referential	non-referential		
	abstract expressionism		**HIGH**
	minimal art		
realist painting ↔	↔ *realistic painting (à la Duval)*		Ideas or Techniques
"Surfacing" ↔	↔ *"Surfacing"*		
Duane Hanson's sculpture ↕	*contemp. surrealist poetry* ↕	*theatre of the absurd* ↕	
Duane Hanson's sculpture	*contemp. surrealist poetry*	*theatre of the absurd*	**LOW**
documentaries	*good escape novels*		Events
contemp. work poems			

The presence of the same example in two areas means there is more than one way the same piece of art is perceived. Good art (and my concern in this critique is with work produced at a high enough level of artistic skill to be generally regarded by the contemporary audience for art as good art) is often powerful enough to resist any easy classification of it, but it is usually *perceived* by a particular viewer or reader as existing inside a certain classification. For example, to many people contemporary realist painting refers to certain objects (that is, these people can make out what is going on in the painting). So this art may be considered referential, and placed on the left-hand side of my chart. At the same time, this type of painting usually has a non-narrative content (it does not deal primarily with events). So we may locate it in the upper-left-hand corner of the chart. But Paul Duval, in his *High Realism in Canada* (Toronto: Clarke, Irwin, 1974) shows through his text that it is possible to perceive the paintings as non-referential as well as non-narrative. Duval's discussion of the paintings is almost entirely about techniques (types of paints used, size of the artist's studio, what light the artist works in, and so on). Virtually nothing is said about the content, and so the work (and the book) moves over into the "fashionable" side of the chart. Similarly, even photorealist paintings may be discussed as the interaction of abstract forms, irrespective of their referential content. For a literary example: many critics have argued that Margaret Atwood's novel *Surfacing* isn't really about four young people going into Quebec, but about how the various characters embody nationhood, feminism, discovery of roots, etc. So the book lands in the upper, or high art, half of the chart, rather than in the low art half where it would be placed if it was perceived primarily as a narrative, an account of certain events. But I have also read reviews and heard discussions that remove the referentiality of the book entirely, and consider it solely in terms of the various concepts discussed (i.e., the book is considered non-referentially, as though it were simply a treatise on certain abstract ideas). And thereby the book is moved into the fashionable side of the ledger, as well.

Duane Hanson is an American sculptor who creates life-sized representations of people, almost resembling mannikins. In his early work Hanson chronicled events (one piece called "Riot" consists of several figures of blacks and police fighting, and one called "Vietnam" shows dead and dying U.S. soldiers). Since then he has moved to single pieces which may be seen as embodying certain static ideas or techniques rather than narratives (a figure of a tired commuter, or a woman shopping). I have seen references to this change as an "improvement", and Hanson is catalogued with the high realists now (i.e. in

Rothman's recent realism exhibit). He has ascended, then, into high art. Let me stress again that I am not concerned here with the artist's *intention* in creating his pieces (which, after all, most critics have no way of knowing) but rather how the work is currently perceived. "Riot" or "Vietnam" *had* to be seen as concerned with events; there was no satisfactory way of discussing only their technique. Whatever Hanson wants for his single figures, though, they have found an acceptance at present as high art, removed from whatever events might have prompted their creation or what events might still be considered to be implicit in these figures.

Examples of some other art forms are found in both the high and low categories of the chart. Surrealist poetry, though always fashionable (i.e. non-referential) now is considered high (the New York school of surrealists) or low (Pablo Neruda) depending on whether or not the poem simply plays with the possibilities of the poetic technique or is perceived as being primarily a response to events. Similarly with theatre of the absurd. On the other hand, some art forms seem immobile. Fashionable, non-referential, technique-obsessed abstract expressionism is always seen as very high art, for example. Good escape novels are locked into a low position. They may be considered non-referential, hence fashionable, because what reference they have is understood by the sophisticated reader to refer not to real objects and actual events but to entirely imaginary ones—ones that never existed except in the writer's mind—even though the novels do have a definite narrative structure. And finally on our chart, down in the lower-left-hand corner we find permanently placed the realist art forms such as the documentary and the contemporary work poem.

The chart, I feel, helps explain my puzzlement at the critical position accorded our realist poets. For built into this diagram, I think, is the *pull* of the upper-right-hand corner. It seems to me that, just as Marx and Engels pointed out, the ruling ideas of any age are the ideas of its ruling class. So in art now there seems to be a tendency among everyone (producers, critics and audience) to see the upper-right-hand corner (the preference of the societal elite that makes up most of the audience for art) as housing the "real" or "serious" art. The other corners meanwhile may be taken as more or less serious depending on their relation to the upper-right-hand corner.

In my own experience as a poet I've encountered that current *pull* of the upper-right-hand corner a number of ways. I sometimes hear the comment from students, academics, and even other poets, "I like your stuff. But it isn't poetry. Poetry is something you can't understand." What is this but a filtering down of the perception that "real" art is found in the high, non-referential corner of the chart? In part this attitude comes from an educational system which still enshrines as its poetic models the work of the English Romantics—a small group of Englishmen who write what is for contemporary North American audiences material that is about the life of a completely different time, place, class and society. And the poems that counter this kind of verse—the modern avant-garde as it were—that are taught are the difficult and extremely cloudy poems of Pound, Eliot, etc. With these given to people as the range of possibilities for poetry, it is no wonder that obscurity and quality are linked in so many people's minds.

The reception given to my anthologies of contemporary North American work poems also demonstrates that lure of the upper-right-hand corner. To the usual college audience for poetry the poems are enjoyed only as a description of what it is like to work at various jobs of which the authors usually aren't particularly enamored. That is, the poems are perceived as about events, referential, low, and hence unimportant. Yet if with these audiences I start speaking about critical theories to do with the modern work poem, I can see ears beginning to perk up: we are entering the world of theory, idea, technique, shifting to the upper portion of the chart. I have a little rap which I have found effective in introducing this audience to the potential richness for criticism of this material.

Basically, as Artem Lozynsky of Temple University first noticed, these poems display a completely different orientation than earlier labor poems. Before the current generation of writers, poems about work are either written from outside the working life altogether (see Jeremy Warburg's *The Industrial Muse* [London: Oxford University Press, 1958]), or, when written by people actually employed at various jobs, the poems usually describe not the details of the job but rather the poet's hopes for the future. It was enough to be working, to be a member of the class that was soon to be ascendent. To discuss the nitty-gritty of any particular job wasn't as important as to express solidarity, progress, a look forward to the great Day that was coming. But within the last decades, all this has changed. Due apparently to the phenomenon of so many young people moving back and forth between technical schools, community colleges, universities and the work force, a substantial body of poetry has been emerging about life at various jobs. These poems are written from *inside* those jobs and express not hope for the future but rather the specific detail of working conditions and of the working lives of the poet and his or her fellow employees. Politically, or sociologically, this change may be seen as demonstrating an awareness that worthwhile social progress will not come from outside the working world, and must concretely alter the material and social relationships on the job for the better. Lozynsky and I call this change in the writing "the abandonment of heaven", since missing entirely from these new poems is any sense that participation in the work force will lead to any particular future, let alone a glorious socialist one. We feel it is an accurate description of the mood of the working world today, not only because of the affirmative response of those in the work force who have been exposed to these poems, but also because the poems seem to reflect accurately the concerns of people working today (for instance, the almost complete absence of positive reference to unions, which previously had inspired some of the most militant and energetic labor verse. This appears to match the usual rank-and-file attitude toward unions on most jobs. The union is seen as a kind of personnel department that is supposed to have something in it for you, but rarely does.).

I can go on and on like that. The religious imagery suggested by the reference to abandonment of belief in a future heaven-on-earth can be extended to some critical classifications of work poems: ones that deal with initiation into the rites and mysteries of particular jobs, ones that deal with the unsatisfying transubstantiation of time and exertion into mere money. And poems about working outdoors often show the poet aware of another order in the universe besides that of the job—the natural order that, for example, a logger-poet is always working *against* in the woods. But the point here is that because of the current *pull* of the upper-right-hand corner of the chart, it is the expounding of theoretical critical concepts like these that sparks the most interest in work poems among the usual audience for poetry. Once these concepts are shown to them, for the first time they begin to feel that perhaps this poetry might have some relation to "real" art, and hence be worth serious consideration.

But to a different audience, one which finds the work poems particularly meaningful, such critical speculation can seem either nonsensical or irrelevant. When the poems are presented to people not particularly familiar with contemporary poetry but to whom the poems are especially referential (for example, when the poems have been used in classes at technical institutes in Canada or at The Labor School in Detroit), there is a tremendous surge of enthusiasm and delight. "I didn't know anyone could write about this", is the repeated comment, and people want to read and buy a book of poems perhaps for the first time in their lives.

And this differing response seems to me to point to a serious flaw in the current perception of art. To a literary critic, whose ordinary world involves mostly handling pieces of paper, a poem which contains a narrative out of the life of a logger appears to speak of a totally alien world. It is a world which is also clearly referred to, and thus one that is uninteresting to somebody in search of what is at present considered "real" art. Understanding the connection between the existence of that logger and the pieces of paper the critic lives among takes a leap of imagination in a direction in which unfortunately the usual critic is neither trained nor inclined to go. The gap between his world and the life of most Canadians is too great. I think of the Toronto writer who responded in genuine puzzlement to the observation that B.C. poet Peter Trower lived much of his life in a logging camp with: "Why would he do that?" Of course, the answer is in the poetry, but Trower's poems are not ordinarily perceived to contain ideas, only events.

Thus I believe my chart on how contemporary art is currently perceived diagrams an alienated perception. It is the perception of people who are cut off either by choice or education (or both) from understanding much about the majority of the population of their country, the people whom they must move among and have dealings with every day. Now, I don't want to suggest that people who have adopted this alienated perception should stop writing. I know I want to keep writing what to me is most important to set down, as in my experience most authors do. But at the same time it bothers me that there is not a single major Canadian novel about the industrial working life that consumes most of the time of most Canadians every day. In searching for novels for an Introduction to Canadian Literature course I was to teach recently, I became aware once again that the overall image this country projects through its fiction is very far away from the Canadian reality. Given my chart on how art is perceived, this is understandable, but no less reprehensible for all that. My own experience with the work poem anthologies is that when poetry begins to speak realistically about the lives of more people, then more people become interested in the art. Thus it seems to me to be advantageous not only to literature, but to all literary artists, that our writing incorporate the conditions of existence of most of us.

Not that simply reaching more people is what I am advocating here; I don't mean to hold up Terry Rowe or Rod McKuen as models. What is important to me is that realism is a means to widen the potential audience for what might be said, adult-to-adult. The German critic T.W. Adorno, in his analysis of the culture industry (*Cinéaste,* Winter 1971-72), cautions that:

> The function of something that concerns numerous individuals is no guarantee of its value. To confuse the aesthetic phenomenon with its vulgarizations does not lead to art as social phenomenon, to its real dimension; but it often serves to defend something that is debatable in its social consequences.

For what is wrong with a national literature that does not deal with the problems, aspirations, failures and successes of the majority of men and women who inhabit the country is that the literature becomes one more means by which people are kept confused as to what is important and what is possible in their lives.

At present everyone finds themselves submerged in a flood of advertising that seeks to define and control our experiences through encouragements to purchase various commodities. And we are also trapped in a deluge of products of the culture industry, products that as we shall see tend to describe and then "solve" problems that are not the difficulties of our daily life (even if the "solutions" proposed were practicable). These are errors of commission. But by inference, or omission, the products of the advertising and culture industries teach us something more pernicious. Since the lives and problems these industries see as fit to deal with are not *our* lives and problems, we learn that our lives and problems are not significant ones. Our daily existence and its difficulties and achievements are not important, not worthy to be considered by the "serious" worlds of money and art. So we learn we are nothing. Speaking of the culture industry as a whole, Adorno points out:

> Its representatives make believe that this industry provides men with something akin to signposts for their orientation in a supposedly chaotic world—and that this reason alone is sufficient to make the culture industry acceptable.

But *is* Canada a nation of people who mainly spend their time obsessed with relationships, who trip about in the backwoods and think deep thoughts about nationhood? *Has* anyone been helped in facing the problems of their everyday world by reading *Surfacing, Bear,* or *For My Brother Jesus?*

Where books like these do tackle actual everyday problems, the effect of our current orientation towards art leads the writers to "enhance" the subject matter by treating it symbolically or mythologically. This creates certain unfortunate results. For one thing, it limits the audience who can understand the books to those who have been educated into reading on more than one level, those able to grasp and interpret symbol and myth. The author becomes a cult-leader, speaking to the converted. A corollary of this is that readers in the know perceive that their job is to "translate" the meaning of the work out of its mythic or symbolic universe. Thus much human attention and ingenuity and thought goes to deal not with the problems to which the author so ingeniously alludes, but to deciphering what the book is in fact about and what the author's "message" is. In many cases, this "message" is banal or otherwise useless as a solution. Yet those of us who are able to get this far are asked not to comment on that banality but rather on the clever way the author has concealed the topic and the lesson in the work.

A further result of this drive to treat daily life symbolically or mythologically is that once again it teaches us that our own problems are not important. What we face in the ordinary, non-symbolic world is not worthy of significant thought. Our experiences, our everyday lives are not to be taken seriously, unless they can be seen as functioning symbolically or mythologically, that is, seen as something *larger* than reality.

Adorno gets quite harsh with those products of a culture industry that hint or claim they offer solutions to non-existent or far-fetched problems unrelated to those difficulties and decisions people must face every day. He refers to:

> the impotence and the lack of substance in the content of that which...(the culture industry)... transmits. Pretending to be the guide for the helpless and deceitfully presenting to them conflicts that they must perforce confuse with their own, the culture industry does not resolve these conflicts except in appearance—its "solutions" would be impossible for them to use to resolve their conflicts in their own lives.
>
> In this industry's productions people enter into difficulties only to get out of them unharmed and, in the majority of cases, with the help of the infinitely good collectivity....

I feel that Adorno's description matches a good deal of the content of current Canadian writing. Even the poems of writers as apparently anti-establishment as Milton Acorn can fall under Adorno's description. Acorn is an author that to me has abandoned a realistic portrait of his world for historical re-creations and writing which offers the tenet of "Canadianism" as a panacea for the ills of modern industrial society. Isn't this nationalist sentimentality just one more variation of that imaginary "infinitely good collectivity" which so much of the culture industry, as Adorno says, offers as an unlikely solution to the problems it defines as important? What use is it to pretend that "independence" or "the Rev" will solve the real problems of daily life, when these problems are only rarely referred to and then in their most romanticized form? Not that social change is impossible; but it must grow from a clear understanding (and hence depiction) of what those daily problems are that the social change is supposed to be able to cure.

Thus I believe we have to examine very carefully all art that says or implies that it is showing us the conditions of our lives. With this in mind, I think realism can be broken down into two distinct categories, not according to how the art is perceived, but according to its content.

The first and oldest mode of realist art, and the least useful I think, is what I consider External Realism. This is our world as described by artists outside what they are depicting. This is a poem about a construction gang written by a poet looking at them through a fence. This is a documentary written about the expulsion of the Japanese from the B.C. coast written by a non-participant who lives in another culture. This is the Russian brand of socialist realism: a glorification or exaggeration of the conditions of the working life, or that life seen as a march with banners and flags toward a glorious Day yet to come. This is the majority of Canadian paintings done inside factories: the painting of munition plants commissioned by the government during World War II.

A famous example of External Realism is the Diego Rivera murals about the auto industry painted in the 1930s at the Detroit Institute of Arts. The murals are a powerful indictment of assembly-line manufacturing. But they are very much art produced from outside the experience they seek to describe. In some panels the employees are presented as virtually faceless, whereas doing factory work is an experience of personalities;

you are always conscious of who specifically is working beside you and what their individual human strengths and shortcomings are. Overall, Rivera's murals show people turned into mindless cogs in an industrial machine. But that is not how it is to actually work in the plants each day. All this art—whatever its aesthetic merits—lacks the accuracy that a participant-artist brings to describing or depicting the situations the art seeks to render. One touchstone I find useful is—is there any humour? Laughter is one important means by which a large percentage of the human race deals with the problems of daily life in industrial society. External Realist art seldom contains humour because an outside artist is in no position to understand what is *particularly* absurd or unusual in the situation being presented. He or she literally doesn't get the joke.

To me, even future-oriented work poetry produced by participants inside the industrial process is a form of External Realism. Instead of seeing what lies about him or her, the poet uses an external ideological framework to try to bend or alter what is happening to fit a preconceived pattern. Much current Chinese-style socialist realism falls into this category. Here is a poem, for example, by Chen An-an, one of the new proletarian poets (from *Thousands of Songs Dedicated to the Party* [*Qian-ge-wan-qu xian-gei dang*; Shanghai: 1971]; quoted in Kai-yu Hsu's *The Chinese Literary Scene* [New York: Vintage, 1975]):

Every Calendar Page, a Victory Poster
(Yenan Machine Casting Factory, Shanghai)

A journey of three thousand miles glowing in red
 sunlight,
Thousands of wood shavings curl up a spring tide
 under the plane,
In long strides we fly across the threshold of 1971,
Every leaf from the calendar a victory poster.

Here the concern of the poet is not to portray accurately the conditions of life working in this factory, but rather to relate to the future-oriented themes of fulfilment of quotas and the parade toward the better life to come.

As opposed to all this, I see a second category of realist art, which I consider to be Internal Realism. So far, I have found this new Internal Realism mainly in writing. The high realist painters, for example, seem to me mostly to stand outside what they portray. They will paint weathered barn boards, but not—even if they have had the experience—the life of a working farmer. For me Internal Realism is art that is us showing ourselves to ourselves: contemporary North American work poems, some of the new feminist writing that relentlessly probes the actual condition of women in our time and place, documentaries made by participants in events themselves. This is art made by those who are *inside* the situations they speak of, when they describe what is around them.

In doing this, an Internal Realist artist naturally loses the "objectivity" of the external, alienated viewpoint. But I feel accuracy and understanding are gained, along with an ability to capture the true range of emotions that are connected with the subject being considered. So I believe the new Internal Realism to be more honest, deeper, richer than the old External Realism. All one has to do is study the differences in the two types of work poems, for instance, to see an immense strengthening of the art both in terms of complexity and aesthetics. As the skills that artists need in order to create filter down from the social groups that formerly had a monopoly on them, I believe we are going to see more and more examples of Internal Realism, in more areas than at present. After all, who can any of us trust to speak for us, except ourselves? The media people, locked into the institutions they serve? The unions, parliamentary representatives, professional radicals, or any other spokesperson for us? Professional artists, who face trying to function in an art world shot through with an alienated perception of what constitutes both reality and art? To detail the problems of our lives, we can rely only on ourselves, speaking as clearly and accurately as we can about what we know to be true.

Further, I feel that the artistic productions of the new Internal Realism are part of what the Preamble to the Constitution of the Industrial Workers of the World calls building the new society "within the shell of the old". For there is a social aspect to this art with implications for social change. First, Internal Realism insists that we must act ourselves, that no "professionals" or "representatives" can do it for us. It says this to the new mother who is trying to write: that unless she spells it out herself how for years she never gets a full night's sleep, that the constant tiredness is as much a companion in her life as her children and husband, it will never get said. It says this to those living every sort of job who want to write: that unless they describe this life it will never get said. And so I believe Internal Realism teaches that no *solution* to these problems will be given to us either. We must make the solutions ourselves, out of all our ugliness and beauty, our irrationality and rationality, our full, real life.

Second, by taking the problems of our daily lives as worthy of serious artistic consideration in and as themselves, Internal Realism does not contribute to the notion that our lives are unimportant, that what happens to us is not as significant as what occurs to the fictitious characters in symbolic or popular art or advertising. So it is my hope that Internal Realism can introduce and/or reinforce the self-confidence we need to reconstruct the world after *our* needs and desires.

Third, Internal Realism through its description of everyday life teaches that in the interconnectedness of all things there is a message of human solidarity. Every object we touch comes to us through the work of another. Behind each thing—the paper I am typing on now, the typewriter I am using, the clothes I wear, the food I just ate—there is both human work and the human existence that sustains that work so grudgingly. What is this society like, that it can drive someone to work every day in a typewriter assembly plant? And what are the conditions society establishes within that plant? In addition to the sound of the keys striking, then, I hear the voices of those who worked on my machine. And I understand the voices most clearly, most accurately, when I get sent to me (as sometimes happens) or read otherwise the first poems written out of that particular occupation. Piece by piece the world fits together, with people changing jobs, moving around, falling in love, having families, retiring, dying. But always at the center of the lives is the work that must be done to get the money to live, and how that work (those hours, conditions, amounts of pay) alters and twists and corrupts and fulfils those of us who go to it every day.

I believe that the appearance and development of the subject of industrial work in our literature is the beginning of the end of the stranglehold that the subjects of love, death and nature presented as though unconnected with daily reality have had on our writing for so long. Much of what can be written about work is brand new. When I write an ordinary love poem, I have to nudge away from the paper the thousands and thousands of poets who have been at this before me, who now come crowding around my desk to see and influence what I'm putting down. But in most jobs, the new poets writing about these lives of theirs are the very first in the history of literature to tackle that particular topic. To me, the new description of a human endeavour is like a gift, a gift linking another part of the daily world to my own. It is this sense of interconnectedness, this message of the referentiality and solidarity of all things and human events, that I believe permits the new Internal Realism to perform in a small way the social function previously provided by a belief in class solidarity. If we understand, and are helped by our art to understand, that we all contribute to the daily rebuilding of the world (except for a few drones like politicians, bosses and bureaucrats) then I think we can better understand that even at present we run the world. All we don't do yet is control it.

I know of no other mode of art besides Internal Realism

that can claim these social functions, and that is why it is so important to me. If all art is mute or not-so-mute testimony to the work that went into (and hence the lives behind) the production of the art, or the production of the materials out of which the art is made, or the production of any object or condition or event referred to in the art, then there can be neither high nor low art. All art can be perceived as being about human events, and referential, even if it is not particularly intended to be so by the artist. So we lose the assumption of the present perception of art that if art is obscure it is deep, and if clearly referential, shallow. We begin to have new virtues for art: clarity, precision, illumination. None of this means to advocate an end to this or that kind of art now fashionable, but it does mean that *as well as* the other kinds of art we want to have and take seriously art that imaginatively and precisely reflects the ordinary working lives of most Canadians.

So what are the limits of realism? I don't know, because I think that with the emergence of the new Internal Realism we have barely begun to comprehend realism's potential, both for art and as a possible factor in social change. As for me, to say that we have barely begun to understand the potential of realism is to say that we have barely started to understand the potential of art itself.

REGIONAL CULTURE, NATIONAL CULTURE, INDUSTRIAL CULTURE

I

At a conference on regional literature held in 1979 at the University of Regina, those of us in attendance had a chance to hear some prominent Canadian writer/academics try to define what constitutes regional literature, and what its value is.

Participants at the conference noted that the hosting of such a gathering at Regina was in itself testimony to the recent rise to consciousness of a vigorous and visible Canadian prairie culture. By "culture" they meant the common, limited definition of the word: productions in any of the fine arts that are expressive in some way of aspects of the lives of a given people in a given era. And this new visibility in prairie culture perhaps accounts for the presence at the conference of some long-time expatriate writer/academics from the region who were also, more generally, returnees to the West. Speaking at Regina were Eli Mandel (born in Estevan, Saskatchewan, who taught since 1967 at York University in Toronto but for 1978-79 was writer-in-residence for the city of Regina) and Robert Kroetsch (born in Heisler, Alberta, who taught since 1961 at the State University of New York in Binghamton but in 1978-79 was teaching at the University of Manitoba). And yet for all that was said by these and other panelists, the two principal questions intended to be dealt with by the conference were largely left unanswered.

It took Ann Wall, the owner of Toronto's House of Anansi Press, to stand in the audience and point out that the existence of a regional culture presupposes the existence of a central, or non-regional culture. For English-speaking Canada, due to the concentration in Toronto of wealth, population, and the head offices and major studios of the nationally-distributed communications and cultural media, the non-regional culture is synonymous with that city. From Wall's observation it is possible to conclude that, just as the various featured conference speakers draw their national intellectual importance from their acceptance by the cultural world of Toronto, so regional culture is that culture which exists *outside* the recognition and approval of that central (Toronto) culture.

As for the worth of regional literature, the conference repeatedly heard—besides some debate as to whether or not Shakespeare was a regional author—that all good writing is important whether or not it is ever recognized as such outside the region where it is written and circulated. What constitutes "good" writing was not considered.

To me, however, the entire discussion missed the most important issue concerning both regional culture and the central culture usually referred to as "Canadian" culture: who participates in the culture—as creator, audience, or subject?

To use literature as an example. A book of poems about aspects of the poet's early life can be published in an edition of

1,000 copies and be hailed in the literary press as a worthy addition to Canadian or, say, prairie culture. But is it? The author, audience, and concerns of the book can be completely removed from the lives of an enormous majority of the inhabitants of the nation or that region. In what sense, then, does such a book have anything to do with a geographic area if most people in that region live a daily life entirely different from the subject of this book?

For me, the touchstone of cultural authenticity has to be a book's (or other cultural artifact's) engagement with the governing experience of everyday life in any region—daily work. After all, the reason people settle in a community, and hence what defines a community, is the work that is available there. This applies whether this community is situated in a geographic locale considered part of a region or the "center" of a country. When regional or central literature ignores daily work, the attempt made by the literature to portray the life of a community moves further and further away from the realities of that community.

Take Ken Mitchell's anthology of Canadian prairie writing, *Horizon* (Toronto: Oxford University Press, 1977). What little reference there is in this collection to the work done on the prairies refers exclusively to the past. The rest of the material suggests, as does much contemporary prairie writing, that prairie life takes place for the purposes of appreciating the prairie landscape and engaging in interpersonal relationships (with both activities completely separated from the effects daily work has on them). Much central, or "Canadian", literature is no different. Consider the topics dealt with by the poems in John Newlove's anthology *Canadian Poetry: The Modern Era* (Toronto: McClelland and Stewart, 1977). If you wanted to show anyone what the life of modern Canadians is like, would you show them this book?

To attempt to portray a region while ignoring the governing daily experience of the people who live in it leaves an author with only the landscape, an imagined history or future, and interpersonal relations to depict. And all of these must be seen with the eye of an *outsider*, since neither the past, the future, nor the work in the present which takes place in the landscape and which so influences those relationships are participated in by the writer. Hence, there is the danger of *other* outsiders (whether expatriates or not) suddenly showing up with better literary "credentials" than local practitioners to take over the task of portraying a region. The local practitioners may feel vaguely put upon by this, but one outsider's view is probably as limited as another's.

This phenomenon is not a distinctly Canadian one. P.J. Laska, an editor of the West Virginia literary magazine *The Unrealist*, has noted (in the 1978 issue) similar events occurring in Appalachia:

> ...we find volunteer ethnics whose search for roots is one of the contemporary responses to the loss of community in capitalist society. In Appalachia, for example, a new Narodnik movement is shaping up as an awakened and aroused "intelligentsia" rushes to embrace the "true folk" of the Region, in whom are said to reside all the decent values quashed in the "outside" world of mass capitalism. The search for a living art which is a form of communication and solidarity leads the volunteer ethnics to the submersion of art in roots, in the illusion of homogeneity and identity in bloodlines rather than experience and struggle. In poetry it leads to a nostalgia verse as dead as the past it idealizes.

Mary Joan Coleman, another *Unrealist* editor, further classifies these actual or psychic returnees:

> On the one hand we have the Slicksters, witty urbanites with prestigious degrees and condescending egos who have come "back to the land" to live high off the hog.... On the other hand, we have the Shucksters, a home-grown species of hustler who thrives on a concentrated diet of volunteer ethnicity. Yet they would not hesitate to walk over top of the downtrodden natives they profess to represent on their way to the headlines of the cash register. In unreality, they are alienated intellectuals and self-interested profiteers who are as cool and pop in most respects as their outsider counterparts.

The central literary culture in Canada is no less vulnerable to outsiders. Certain literary ideas of famous American, British, or other outsiders to the daily experiences of other peoples constantly sweep through the Toronto literary scene, hold sway for a time, and then are replaced. The literary "nationalists" may grumble, but they are as helpless to prevent it as any of Coleman's Appalachian "Shucksters".

But whether the Canadian counterparts to the types identified by Laska and Coleman intend to present the life of a particular region or the country as a whole, the culture they offer hides not only the work people do but also the resultant fact that the people of any community or region or nation are divided into employers and employees—and in farming areas, into the landless and the landowners. And, as the Preamble to the Constitution of the Industrial Workers of the World says:

> The working class and the employing class have nothing in common.

Thus the so-called regional or national cultures can be seen as one more attempt to obscure this fundamental dichotomy in the inhabitants of a geographic locale. The pretense is that those with economic control over their fellow citizens (the power to hire and fire) and those who are employed for a living have something in common: a culture. Recent events in Quebec provide the perfect example of the consequences of such a notion. The White Paper produced by the Parti Quebecois government listing the wrongs suffered by Quebec and the PQ's proposals to cure these social ills does not mention that *within* French-speaking Quebec there is also a fundamental difference of interest between French-speaking bosses and French-speaking employees. The conditions of daily work in Quebec are not part of the Quebecois culture that the PQ government wishes readers of its White Paper to ponder.

Or, for a less theoretical example: in the Fall of 1979 I was in Montreal speaking with college teachers at a CEGEP. Their union is part of a united front of government employees which was at that time locked in battle with the PQ government over various issues to do with daily work. The unions know the government is their employer, with whom they must fight for improvements in the quality of their working lives. But there is a great deal of support for the PQ among the unions' membership. So much support, in fact, that instead of planning to strike at the moment when the government would be most vulnerable—during the PQ's referendum campaign set for the Spring of 1980—the unions decided to strike in the Fall to let their grievances be settled and out of the way before the PQ had to go to the electorate at large with the sovereignty-association proposals. In short, many members of the united front unions believed they had something in common with their employer: a "national culture" shared by all French-speaking Quebecois. The PQ government, of course, had no such illusions. They understood perfectly their position as employers, and quickly passed emergency legislation outlawing the previously-legal strike and thus smashing that specific effort by the unions to better their members' daily working lives.

Even the much-touted "regional" *landscapes* of Canada are perceived very differently according to an observer's economic relationship to them. Landscapes are obviously not viewed the same by a land developer and a subdivision tenant, by an agribusinessman and a farmer, by a farmer and a hired hand, by an executive of a resource development corporation and an employee of that corporation. There is a fundamental difference between one who idly looks at a landscape and/or who owns it, and one who has to work in that landscape.

Yet most regional or central Canadian culture denies the existence and conditions of our everyday working lives. A glance at the economic basis of this culture shows this is hardly surprising. The bulk of this culture, including the publishers of this book, is subsidized directly or indirectly by the government, by business, by the wealthy. It is not that there is some plot, or some secret censorship board, that induces or coerces Canadian writers, artists, reviewers, etc. to produce this kind of culture. It is just that somehow, in some way, those who bankroll the culture usually get what they pay for.

An interview with Margaret Atwood in the *American Poetry Review* (Sept./Oct. 1979 issue) offers this exchange:

> Karla Hammond:
> "The duty of the critic is to society, but the primary duty of the writer is to the thing being made" (Atwood). Can you elaborate?
>
> Margaret Atwood:
> It's a statement about writing derived from my own background and the fact that Canada is a very political country where people frequently indicate what they feel writers *ought* to be doing. You always have to say first that a writer is a writer....If they're a bad writer—regardless of the attractiveness of their ideas—they're still a bad writer.

But even a "good" writer's productions serve the interest of one class or the other. For example, most contemporary Canadian writing does not provide its audience with an examination of the economic realities of their lives, and the attendant effects of these realities on their loves, hates, appreciation of nature, and so on. Instead, the writing offers escape: either escape into a narrative usually situated far removed from the reader's day-to-day existence, or else escape into the world of high art—play with interesting, astonishing, or boring arrangements of words and images. Most contemporary Canadian writers display no interest as to *why* people in our society want to escape from their daily lives. The concept that everyday existence could be fulfilling is equated in our literature only with brief moments of romantic love (in which moments, characteristically, the people involved have no past and no connection with the present society around them; they enter a world of "just we two", as the song has it).

The creation of a literature, however "good", that fulfils the social role of providing escape from everyday reality serves the interests of a class which is not keen on much self-examination by participants in that everyday reality. The "good" writer may think he or she is merely fulfilling their "duty to the thing being made". But in doing so, he or she is also fulfilling a duty to the boss.

Writing like this which ignores the major realities of Canadian life does one of the same jobs as commercial advertising: it causes working people to disappear. Just as few people actually work in the artifacts of the official culture, so it is rare that any representation of the working world appears in advertising. In the infrequent instances that this does happen, its function is merely to provide a useful image. One example is the recent advertising campaign which featured a model supposedly "Feeling Satisfied" as he smokes a certain brand of cigarette, while apparently working on the B.C. booming ground depicted in the background of the ad. Clearly this is a fantasy, like the clean-fingernailed Marlboro model who could not possibly be the real working cowhand suggested by his outfit.

But the *effect* of this absence of actual working lives in our culture is illustrated in a letter to me from Ron Cronkhite, a young man who has written some poems about his employment in a Chrysler plant in Windsor, Ontario. The experience Cronkhite describes is partly the result of the conditions of that work, and partly occurs because in our society to be a "factory worker" means to be invisible:

> It is impossible for one to identify with his factory work and become anything other than what is commonly called a 'burn-out' (we all know a few of these—don't we?). So everyone seems to push their work to the peripheral areas of their identity. Rather than 'factory workers', it seems to be the case to an astonishing degree that you have factories manned by other people. Ask them what they are, they're 'farmers' who work at the factory, or 'carpet salesmen' who work in the plant, or 'Jesus freaks' or 'acid heads' or 'athletes' or anything but 'factory workers' who work in the factories.

What more could the boss class expect from its "good" writers than that these writers help create a situation where the *idea* of classes, the very concept of being employed in a factory, disappears from those who are actually doing that work?

A second function that the official culture shares with commercial advertising is the depiction of an unreal present. Just as no one lives, or talks, or thinks the way characters in advertising do, so the concerns of contemporary writing are usually a long distance away from the daily concerns of most Canadians. But the pernicious fact is that if the advertising is effective enough and/or the literature is "good" enough, an audience or readership may be seduced into taking these other concerns for their own. So instead of thinking about ways to act to improve our daily working reality, we begin to worry about how our armpits smell, or about "national unity", or if Christianity as interpreted by a particular poet is responsible for the ills of Western man. Again, what could please the boss class more than a literature which turns people away from an examination and eventual improvement of their own daily lives? What more could the bosses want from writers than that they lead people towards consideration of intellectual fads, impossible difficulties gotten into by impossible characters, or, more generally, imaginary solutions to imaginary problems?

But it is not my intention to advocate censoring any kind of writing. Human freedom is what the struggle for a better life is all about, and cultural freedom is no less important than economic freedom. Also, it should be obvious by now that in art as in science it is the freedom to work on seemingly irrelevant problems that sometimes leads to solutions to the most practical questions that arise. Nor am I trying to say that there is only one possible topic for art. Every artist and every member of his or her audience likes to sample a range of subjects, a range of moods.

As well, there exists today a literature at the edge of work that demonstrates the same skilful and accurate examination of aspects of contemporary life that the new writing about work does. Some of the pioneering feminist, native Indian, black, and Chicano writing on this continent have contributed in their way to the ferment for change that is associated with an insider's expression of previously unwritten lives. In addition there are collections of poems that present after-work situations written by participants accurately, richly. As an example, I think of two productions of Thistledown Press in Saskatoon: Glen Sorestad's *Prairie Pub Poems* (1976; accounts of the prairie past, present and future observed through the prism of the ubiquitous small town beer parlor) and Stephen Scriver's *Between the Lines* (1977; poems about the life of a serious amateur hockey team from Grenfell, Saskatchewan).

Yet let us see clearly what effect the overwhelmingly-escapist content of our contemporary culture has on our society. Escape may be fine if it is balanced by reality, but if the *core* of our art is escape there is surely something wrong. Art cannot exist without experiment and play. But if experiment and play constitute most of a people's art then art for these people is mainly a game played by a few for the amusement of a few (and to the detriment of the many).

Let us recognize that there is another potential for literature than this, one that is not so confusing or harmful to people. To be specific in just one area of Canadian literature: myths. A number of writers, apparently feeling that contemporary life is not baffling enough, have consciously set out to invent literary myths for their readers to occupy themselves by trying to decipher.

Robert Kroetsch, for instance, has attempted in a recent novel to express his vision of the Canadian prairies by inventing a mythic occurrence in which a woman is raped by a swarm of bees. By the writing and publication of this, plus his statements about it in interviews, Kroetsch has encouraged his audience to ponder the mythic significance and implications of this. But meanwhile, on the same prairie, entirely different myths are in actual circulation, believed in by flesh and blood human beings *to their cost.* Time and energy spent considering what Kroetsch puts forward for our examination confuses prairie reality with one man's fantasy. The oil that through its royalties helps pay for some of the growth in prairie writing is drilled by young men working 14, 12-hour days in a row—a government-sanctioned, industry-wide violation of existing labor laws (see the *Edmonton Journal*, Dec. 14, 1979). The resultant toll has been terrible: 19 killed in 1979, with hundreds more maimed for life, and lost-time accidents approaching 5,000. Why does this happen? It occurs in part because of the myth of the roughneck, the myth of quick money, and the myths of what that money can buy. These are extant myths that lure a steady succession of young men to the rigs. And so the study where Kroetsch writes his diversions comes to be heated by oil brought to him courtesy of the mangled bodies and hammered lives of those who believe in myths—but actual, living myths, not literary ones. To find a discussion of the dimensions of the existing myths, and what they mean in human terms, we have to go to the oil patch poems of Peter Christensen and the other men and women at work on the rigs who through their writings let both their fellow employees and the rest of us see the cost of oil never figured in the official pronouncements about price-per-barrel.

The white-collar world that Kroetsch and other writer/academics actually work and live in has its own myths, too. These also are often destructive of human lives in their own way, though they are rarely fatal. But myths about how literature is created, about the importance of literature to our culture and of culture to our lives, and about the usefulness of the procedures by which literature is taught are all incorporated into a standard university program of English instruction. How these myths developed, and their effects on human beings who believe in them, could be part of a literature that does not contribute to an obscuring of or an escape from our present Canadian reality.

II

Since today a majority of adult Canadians never read a Canadian book, see a Canadian play, hear a Canadian orchestra or watch a Canadian ballet, let's consider the cultural world most of us do inhabit. I refer to "culture" here in its broadest or anthropological definition: the mental and physical constructs produced by a society. I believe there are two aspects to this larger cultural world. The first is imposed on us, and is all-pervasive, insistent; the second is a culture which we have some hand in originating, and which is no less present, but suppressed.

The culture constantly imposed on us is of course that of the mass consumer society—the cars and entertainment and architecture and household goods and clothes and services that we often help produce at our jobs but which involve somebody else's ideas and which come to us pumped on a flood of advertising, gimmicks, hucksterism. This culture belongs exclusively to the boss; our part in it is mainly as purchaser and consumer. If at work we create a portion of it, this is done according to limits and definitions determined by someone else.

This culture insists it exists for our benefit, to make our lives more pleasurable. And its products do sometimes provide a physical improvement in the quality of our lives, at least until these products break down or are seen to cause other problems for us, or for society, or for the environment. But meantime our very possession of the artifacts of this culture can also be a trap: tying us to a job to pay off first the initial costs of some artifact and then the costs of its inevitably needed replacement.

Furthermore, this culture tries as hard as it can to deny that we have any part in the making of it. As already noted, working people seldom appear in mass consumption advertising. When supposed representatives of our lives appear in entertainment, it is only in grotesque, romanticized, or trivialized forms. Ask any lawyer, for instance, if he or she is able to devote all his or her effort to one case at a time as the lawyers portrayed on TV do. We are thus encouraged by the mass consumption culture to believe that goods and services appear in the marketplace with no social history, produced by magic and not through the thought and labor of others like ourselves. The impression that is created is that other people do not sell their time like we do, but instead are pleased to be allowed to be waitresses or supermarket checkout clerks, for example.

But we know we work for a living. And so we live in another culture, which even more than the mass consumption culture informs our lives and yet which officially is not supposed to exist. I refer here to the industrial culture.

This is the culture which arises from going to work each day in a modern industrial society. It is the sea we swim in. Whether we work on assembly—the paradigm on which nearly all jobs in our society are based—or we work in a classroom or an office we know certain attitudes and activities will be expected of us by the boss. And we also know that at each job our fellow employees will have won some rights and privileges, whether sanctioned by union contract or not, that attempt to restore to us a measure of the humanity that selling our time, our hands, our brains takes away from us.

One part of the industrial culture is thus what the boss contributes: the wage system; the factory system; ugly, noisy workplaces; insufficient or expensive mass transit; a constant pool of unemployed; labor laws and the selective enforcement of these; and so on. The other part is what we do in *response* to the work world established by the bosses, and also what we *initiate* ourselves, to try to make tolerable and to humanize the workplace and the working life. This is the part of the industrial culture where we have the potential to be creative and self-defining. How and where to get hired; how to conduct yourself toward your fellow employees, toward the foreman; whether the crew drinks together after work or disperses; attitudes toward production and/or the company and/or the union; the use of tools and their care; under what circumstances to quit, to walk off, request a transfer; the free space of plant washrooms—all these vary in detail from job to job and yet often are so similar overall in any set of circumstances as to constitute a cultural environment we can be sure of and hence feel part of and contribute to.

Specific differences from occupation to occupation and workplace to workplace make this culture in some ways a rich one—if we are able through circumstance to move from job to job and so sample a little of the variety of this culture.

Otherwise we are forced to settle into one trade, or even one plant or shop or educational institution or office, and find what variety we can in the faces and lives that come and go around us. At the same time, there are enough similarities in how modern work is organized to enable us to be replacement parts in many different occupations.

Working beside immigrants, for example, we learn that one can be employed at many jobs in places where one doesn't even speak the language. And yet each plant and each occupation has its own jargon—part of the diversity of this culture. Depending on where we are, we might use a variety of words not part of ordinary speech: "toolpush", "zapstrap", "hook tender", "fifth wheel", "gangs in the barn", "government work", and/or the ubiquitous numbers that can signify assembly parts, job processes, people being paged, courses taught, and much, much more.

Within the unity and diversity of this culture, not all of us respond to the work world in a similar way, any more than a room full of people respond to watching a ballet in a similar way. For instance, many plants in the 1970s had about a one-third/two-thirds split in them between those who were sometimes called "longhairs" and those known as "lifers". The former were people (often young) who had no particular commitment to the job but were working for money to obtain reasonably immediate goals such as to pay off debts, take a vacation, buy land or a new transmission, and so on. "Lifers" are people (often with families) who whether by choice or necessity have a deeper commitment to remaining at a specific job for a much longer time.

Peter Clecak, of the program in comparative culture of the University of California at Irvine, has written in an essay called *Notes on Work (Antioch Review,* Fall 1978 issue) of the "kaleidoscopic occupational world" of today. With people of so many lifestyles and backgrounds jostling together on the job and exchanging views and perceptions, Clecak says,

> every permutation of work as salvation and damnation becomes a permanent possibility, an attitude individuals may try on and reject immediately—or buy, alter, wear and discard like so many coats on a rack.

Whether we are a diverse group of English professors or of factory hands, however, where we work affects every part of our lives, including our reactions to the mass consumption culture. How much money we have, how we feel at the end of the shift or the week, what the job demands of us physically or mentally, how our fellow employees live and what they talk about, etc., all influence our response to being a consumer. As just one example, in my experience English professors are less likely than factory hands to purchase muscle cars, and factory hands less likely to purchase fantastically expensive stereo systems. Yet such exaggerated consumption for enjoyment and self-enhancement off the job reflects the same lack of personal satisfaction at work—whether due to the routines of factory life or the increasing compartmentalization and bureaucratization of contemporary university teaching. This lack of satisfaction (in individually varying degrees) is an aspect of the industrial culture both groups share.

The part of the industrial culture we originate—for instance, the extent to which we organize the job despite the intentions of the boss and his experts, or the names for people and things we invent—has always been transmitted orally. It is a culture we carry in our heads, passing it on to each other in conversation, jokes, advice, and opinions that in turn lead to various on-the-job actions, or lack of action, and ways we conduct ourselves off work. With the almost total absence of reference to the actual work world in both the official (fine arts) culture and the mass consumption culture, this part of the industrial culture has been the shared possession of working men and women, often unrecognized for what it is even by ourselves. Even the great union hymns of the early struggles for unionism and socialism are mainly about issues like solidarity and martyrdom and the future promised by the struggle rather than about the day-to-day working existence.

But in the past 20 years or so there has begun to appear in print the expanding body of literature about the contemporary working life written by people with first-hand experience of the work they describe. This writing moves the industrial culture out of an oral phase into a written one. Most participants in this culture are excited to see this facet of our lives breaking into print, but as always with an oral culture there are some guardians of it who wish to delay the transition. One of the London organizations that is part of the new British Federation of Worker Writers And Community Publishers reports the censorship by a trade union local of a written account by a worker of his job (from the Federation's anthology *Writing*, 1978):

> Intended for a book on contemporary working lives, some of the content was seen as weakening the union's position by revealing the extent to which workers were able to manage their own jobs at the workplace, instituting their own rules, conditions, breaks and labour-saving methods. We accepted the union arguments, but feel that the time must come when the need to write honestly about work—the major shaping experience in most lives—must overcome expedient reticence. Or are we to accept forever that work is a taboo subject, left to sociological studies or thirty-second television interviews following a strike or serious industrial accident: 'Tell me, Bill, what's it like in there?'.

The increase in writing about the job by participants now

seems irreversible, though. As I mention above in "The Limits Of Realism", the emergence of this material seems to have paralleled in North America the spread of mass public education. And the most visible imaginative writing about the working life—as opposed to written, or tape-recorded and transcribed, work-accounts—is the new work poetry.

These poems arise out of a large and growing range of occupations: blue-collar and white-collar, paid and unpaid labor. They are found here and there throughout this continent's literary magazines and anthologies, and also appear in specialized and individual author's collections, for instance: Jim Daniels' book of Ford assembly line poems, *On the Line* (Bellingham, WA: Signpost Press, 1981); David Conn's Vancouver shipyard poems, *Ticket Stubs for the Bullgang* (Vancouver: Caitlin Press, 1980); the San Francisco longshore Waterfront Writers and Artists' anthology of poetry and fiction, edited by Robert Carson, *The Waterfront Writers: The Literature of Work* (San Francisco: Harper & Row, 1979); or my anthology of job poetry, *Going For Coffee* (Madeira Park, B.C.: Harbour, 1981). Plus, the writers may be heard at readings organized by such groups as the Vancouver Industrial Writers' Union or Emanuel Fried's Buffalo (N.Y.) Labor Writers Workshop.

The new work poems (and the accompanying short stories and plays on similar themes) are the first consciously artistic productions of the contemporary industrial culture. It is precisely these poems (and fictions) that have the potential of introducing into what is currently considered the official culture some sense of how Canadians actually live, think, dream. With regard to the issue of regionalism in Canadian literature, for example, it follows that a literature originating in the working lives of those engaged in the dominant industries of a geographic region probably best captures the essence of that specific place. After all, this is the regional component of the industrial culture. Many jobs are done everywhere, but in certain regions or communities a particular industry can markedly affect the lives of people with no direct association with that industry, i.e., farming on the prairies, logging in B.C., auto assembly in Windsor.

We might ask why *poetry* should appear as the present vanguard of artistic expression of the industrial culture. I think people probably turn to poetry because an exposure to contemporary poetry at some point demonstrated that modern poems can be short, concise, unrhymed, anecdotal—exactly like the conversations in which the industrial culture itself is transmitted. People whose daily work leaves them without time, energy, or self-confidence for longer forms find contempory poetry a handy vehicle to express what they feel is important about their lives.

Poetry is also a non-commercial art form in our society. Because there is no money to be made from it, it is considered within the mass consumption culture to have little, if any, consequence. Money talks, not poetry. Perhaps it is no wonder, then, that people considered to be invisible themselves in the eyes of the mass consumption culture and the official culture choose to embrace an art form also regarded as without importance. With fiction, or other art forms which have the *potential* at least of making money, there is always the temptation to falsify, trivialize, or otherwise alter one's own experiences into a shape that is useable (saleable) by the mass consumption culture. Gene Dennis, one of the most skilful poets and fiction writers of the San Francisco Waterfront Writers and Artists, relates in an interview with Tamin Ansary in 1978 that he once worked on a screenplay for a number of years that was based on a real incident at work. However, Dennis says,

> there was this idea that the function of it was to sell it to Hollywood, and that idea wrote the screenplay. I put a lot of gratuitous sex and violence into it.

Since his association with other dock worker writers, Dennis reports,

> I've been drawing a lot more on my own experiences, my reactions to the work and to changes in the work, my relationships with the other guys. The Waterfront Writers gives me an incentive to come to terms with these things.

The contemporary work poems' willingness to bring into literature all the previously missing detail of how we experience the daily working life represents in addition what is new in contemporary poetry. Fifty or 60 years ago, what was new in poetry were certain experiments in form—including surrealism, sound poetry, automatic writing, the unconventional rearrangement of words on the page. Some writers today still imagine that what was startling half a century ago must remain the path to the future. But in our time the new in poetry is to be found rather in content, specifically this content.

But the value of the new industrial literature is not just this. The British critic David Meakin suggests, in his *Man & Work: Literature and Culture in Industrial Society* (London: Methuen, 1976), a consideration of the daily working life via any medium or genre offers the most significant examination possible of the realities of a society:

> It will be obvious that the nature of work and its status in any given culture affords us an invaluable key to the understanding of that culture as a whole; it is in no case a peripheral, but always a central issue. Industrial civilization, creating forms of work, also creates forms of culture, and it limits our understanding if we utterly dissociate the two. The impoverishment of popular culture is inextricably linked with the

> impoverishment of work in our society, and if we wish to change the one we must change the other as well.

Because the lives the new work writing describes so carefully, so humorously, so bitterly often fall short of a full human existence, I believe this literature implies a call for the social change referred to by Meakin that will improve everyday life. Whatever the immediate intention of the individual work poet, fiction writer or dramatist, the emphasis in their writing on the detail of our present-day working existence says both: "Look at our lives" and "We can do better than this". Taken in its entirety, the new industrial literature even offers by negative inference a glimpse of what a better producing life might be like.

I feel the new work writing also can contribute to such change. Of course a poem or story is an artifact: it cannot do the work of rebuilding the world that people must do. But this writing teaches us that we are important, that our concerns and lives are significant, that we have a right and the ability to make a better daily life than what we have been given. And as the new literature reveals the work we all do that has been hidden from us by the prevailing cultures, the writing also reveals the potential solidarity between all those who share our experiences as employees.

When we sell our time at the job, someone else then "owns" our time; within certain limits, it is the bosses' to do with as they want. But we are not disconnected from our time. We either have to pretend we are, and so drift through the working day by imagining we are somewhere else, daydreaming, or we have to admit that the central and governing hours of our daily life are not our own.

The wage system involves further irrationalities. No one has yet managed to invent a sweat-meter or a brain-meter to determine a standardized, rational rate of remuneration for work done. So each person in our society who works the same eight hours is paid at widely-varying rates, with an elaborate set of often-contradictory arguments used to justify the status quo. Then there is the issue of whose economic losses at the workplace create the bosses' profits.

No amount of writing after work can change all this. But I believe the poems and other work literature can help us understand each detail of what is being done to us, as well as understand the fundamental value of our daily work. The new writing thus contributes knowledge, perspective and encouragement to the struggle to transform the work experience.

To David Meakin, this struggle is absolutely crucial. He feels the fate of democracy itself, no less than culture, hinges on it.

> The whole future of both culture and democracy is at stake. Culture, because when separated from work it becomes gratuitous and socially divisive, a luxury for the happy few. Democracy, because the undermining of creativity in industrial work must inevitably have a corresponding influence on life as a whole, not least on political life. To strip a man of all responsibility in his work is to encourage a lack of responsibility in the whole of his life, it is to promote apathy and thereby to put more and more in jeopardy the real basis of democratic society. To strip him of creativity in his job is to invite a passive attitude toward history, and, therefore, towards the formation of his own life and his own society. To take away that sense of finality in work that hardly seems able to survive the extreme division of labour and the competitive consumer industry of our civilization only contributes to make man less of a member of a meaningful community—worst of

> all, it undermines the very notion of community as an ethical entity with a common sense of purpose.

It is hardly necessary to emphasize that Meakin's comments apply to *any* work situation organized along the lines of the modern wage and/or factory system, whether such a workplace is owned or managed by a modern corporation or any of the contemporary "workers'" or "socialist" states. What Meakin is talking about are the effects on human beings of the prevalent conditions of daily labor on the factory floor, at the desk, or behind the counter virtually anywhere in the world.

And when avenues of expression of the desire for a qualitatively different daily life are blocked—whether by the media, the trade unions, educational institutions, or government "representatives"—it seems one place this wish finds its outlet for the present is in the critique of our contemporary working existence contained in the new industrial literature.

Directly or by implication this writing insists our work is our life, our culture, our country. It also asks, with a sense of humor as often as of outrage: but are we free at work? Do we have a right to be free there—as we are told we have a right to be free before and after work? What are we going to do about it?

THE ENEMIES OF INTELLIGENCE

Further light on the significance of the new industrial literature is shed, I believe, by looking at certain specific responses to the contemporary work poems. Interest and pleasure are the immediate reactions among most audiences. For many people, this material serves as a catalyst for a fresh consideration of their own working lives, just as the early feminist writing provides an opportunity and inspiration for its audience to re-examine their personal circumstances. Some people have also expressed to me a feeling of relief after reading or hearing these poems, as for the first time literature speaks about topics with which they are familiar. Art ceases to be about other places, other eras, other lives. And so these people realize that if art can be about them they too could be artists.

The poems thus have proven popular among adult educators and high school teachers concerned with making literature more approachable and meaningful for their students. (And an astonishing number of school teachers write poems about their work.) Sociologists and labor historians seem intrigued by the poems as well, perhaps recognizing in the poets something of the "participant-observer" of their own disciplines. Working members of the various communications media also have responded favorably to the poems, apparently seeing in them something of that combination of creativity and a daily grind which constitutes the conditions of their own employment.

The contemporary work poems have met with less positive reactions from two directions, however. One source of antagonism towards the poems consists of members of authoritarian left-wing groups. The poems' tight focus on the details of the contemporary working life strongly implies that any beneficial social change must tangibly improve what happens on the job, and in the daily existence the job so influences. Thus this writing does not praise any particular *political* scheme.

In this way the poems are non-political, in the exact sense that the Industrial Workers of the World has always called itself non-political. The I.W.W. is committed to the abolition of the wage system as a means of organizing production, and to the creation of a freer, more democratic social order. But it has always maintained that since the basis of our present society is economic, so opposition to that society must function where society is reproduced daily—on the job. By remaining non-political, the I.W.W. feels it functions in the best manner possible to unite the diverse parts of the working population to improve the working life. Everyone has had the experience of being employed with people we dislike, whose opinions (political, cultural, sporting or otherwise) we disagree with. Yet we are able to fight together with these people against the boss to further our common economic goals and to gain concessions which humanize the workplace. Similarly, the concentration on the problems and delights of the present in the new working poems emphasizes the existence we share, and so suggests the desirability of social change that would alter how we live for the better. But the poems have nothing to do with this or that group of politicians who yearn to exercise state power "on behalf of" or "in the name of" the rest of us.

Most politicians, including left-wing ones, appear to regard themselves as an elite called upon to lead the rest of us into an already-blueprinted future. Hence these people grasp right away that the new industrial literature offers a threat to their ambition. The new writing and its content demonstrates that we who are employed are not dumb in any sense of the word, but capable of expressing for ouselves the conditions of our own life and the kinds of improvements we would like to enjoy. We don't need people to "explain" us, or to tell us what we want. The poems speak against elites of every sort by showing that the work of all of us is necessary for this society to function. Hence, the ideas and actions of each of us are *equally* necessary in order to create a better daily life.

Authoritarian left-wing groups are especially unable to hear working Canadians when, based on our experiences as participants in advanced industrial processes, we express in various ways a desire both for more of the good things of life now and control over our own destiny. Such statements are anathema to organizations dedicated to offering working people "proletarian discipline", the puritan joys of personal deprivation, plus the management of society by a hierarchical band of professional revolutionaries. As "Michael Velli" (Lorraine and Fredy Perlman) has outlined in *Manual for Revolutionary Leaders* (Detroit: Black & Red, 1974), this offering has proven to be more readily acceptable in Third World countries whose citizens are mostly far removed from participation in modern industrial society. Hence the North American authoritarian left's strong identification with Third World movements, struggles and personalities, and the left's characterization of North American employees as "bourgeois". As the Perlmans show, such a characterization is literally nonsense. In Marxist terms, North American working people could only become "bourgeois" at the moment they possess the means and machinery of production. What has occurred instead is the continual development of industrial processes which have resulted in working people expressing a set of desires differently—and in some cases different—than in the era of Marx and Lenin. Stuck in a time warp among early revolutionary literature, however, the hierarchical left cannot hear these contemporary voices. These are voices which in any case dismiss the idea of the necessity of a political vanguard which must rule in the name of working people, as if we are too dull to organize and run society ourselves without their constant direction. The fate of authentic organizations of working people in those states where a vanguard Party holds sway is too dismal and apparently too well known (most recently in the suppression of the Solidarity free trade union movement in Poland) to let the arguments of the authoritarian left capture the imaginations of a majority of working Canadians.

Yet the future is precious to any group conscious of its present weakness. So the refusal of the new work poems to adopt a future vision equivalent to the political left's is taken as an affront. One of the left's authorities, however, seems to have sided with the contemporary industrial authors. Frederick Engels, in a letter from 1885 (quoted in Baxandall and Morawski, eds., *Marx/Engels on Literature and Art* [New York: International General, 1974]), says:

> ...the writer is not obliged to offer to the reader the future historical solution of the social conflicts he depicts.

As if a writer could be that accurate a forecaster! In any event, it would be presumptuous to pretend we know precisely what form the future should have. After all, this is what commercial advertising does. Advertising offers an imaginary future which we are assured is ours if only we buy some specific object or service. In so doing, such advertising as already noted tries to turn us away from concern with our own daily lives, and invites us to live in a supposedly better, unreal world.

The new work literature declines to advertise. It delineates where we are. I feel it is bosses of every type—current or potential—who don't like us to see where we stand, who don't like us to think intelligently about the here and now. If daily existence must be referred to, such rulers prefer duly appointed official or "people's" poets to offer in approved form the content favored by the "leadership". The job of these poets is to speak *for* the officially-silent and officially-stupid whose own testimony about their lives might well contradict approved definitions of reality.

Thus some people on the left find difficulty even with the new industrial literature's description of conditions in today's work world. They would prefer this writing to show the situation at the jobs as their particular group defines these conditions. As they see it, we who work must be portrayed as engaged in militant struggle at the workplace (unconsciously, of course, until a member of their group comes along to explain to us the correct manner to do this).

Such a description is not what they find in the contemporary work poems. This writing reveals human beings surviving through our own ingenious methods in a work environment designed to reduce or abolish our humanity, or at least our adulthood. There is plenty of fight described in these poems. Indeed, the poems themselves may be seen as part of the battle: an act of creation occurring despite every pressure to mutely endure a non-creative existence. But like everything else in these poems, the fight here is seen with an *insider's* eye. That eye observes that resistance may spring out of the oppression that is daily, hourly boredom as well as out of the more dramatic oppression of, say, poor wages or unsafe working conditions. A more obvious, organized, externally-recognizable resistance gets written about too—as long as it actually exists. But the reality at present is that the struggle for survival on most jobs goes on in a manner and in locations that outsiders can't see. The work poems thus teach that it is *our* fight, and , again, it is a fight which must result in the continual improvement of the smallest of the day-to-day conditions here inside our working lives if it is a struggle we may ever consider won.

Another problem the authoritarian left has with the new work literature is the educational level of a number of its practitioners. Some, though by no means all, of the new industrial poets have a college education. This is hardly surprising; the U.S. Bureau of Labor Statistics reported in 1980 that more than one of every three employees over 18 years old had finished at least one year of college. This compared to only 25 per cent of the work force with a year of college in 1970. But a college education is enough to invalidate any of these writers in the eyes of people who prefer to cling to the image of the "real worker" as someone inarticulate and slow-witted. This image always was false. And it is false now.

What we are witnessing in North America is partly the result of working men and women who saved and went without so their children could attend university. As a percentage of the working class went to college, an expectation of their parents was that the educated children would escape from the harsher aspects of the working life. But for various reasons, numbers of these college-trained young people either had to return to the work world of their parents or else have retained wherever they are employed a sense of themselves as employees. And, using skills they gained in their studies, some among these people have begun writing about the working life they are part of, and encouraging others—college-educated or not—to do the same.

Still, the concept of an increasingly college-trained work

force seems to disturb many on the left. The idea disrupts their sense of historical validity; they find the presence within the work world of articulate, artistic men and women to be unacceptable. Technical training in industry is permissible, is desirable, for employees in their view. But technical training in self-expression, in the arts, is definitely not. For the authoritarian revolutionary's dreams of power to come true, working men and women must be an incapable, faceless mass. Should anyone feel the need for a personality, the organization will provide an exemplary Leader (usually male) whose personality can be studied and emulated. But the contemporary work authors instead portray what actually happens to people amid the conditions of the North American work world. This description does not match what the authoritarian left needs to believe goes on here.

So the industrial authors must be discredited: especially if they are educated, what they say must not be true.

And in those cases where work writers—college-trained or not—originate from professional or business families, the authoritarian left has attempted to disparage what they write by evoking the feudal notion of determining one's social position by one's birth. Again this is a consequence of the left-wing politicians' inability to hear what the industrialized employees of their own society are saying and the left's resultant attraction to Third World social movements. Lorraine and Fredy Perlman discuss the problem facing authoritarian revolutionaries of how to apply a political language which evolved from conditions in an industrial country to societies where a majority of the citizens are not involved in modern industrial processes.

> Unlike the feudal champions of the bourgeoisie, the modern champions of the colonized consider themselves members of the oppressed class. In order to do this they find it necessary to overturn capitalist forms of social status and to reintroduce

> class distinctions based on social origin. Capitalism had abolished such distinctions and had replaced them with class distinctions based on social activity, on one's relation to the productive forces. It becomes necessary to overturn the capitalist standard if such social categories as "working class intellectuals" and "proletarian generals" are to become meaningful again.

In the semantic never-never land of the authoritarian left, as the Perlmans point out, "class consciousness" is defined as agreeing with the program of a specific group of left-wing politicians, an (often-peasant) Red Army is considered to constitute the real "proletariat" of a Third World country, while the industrial work force (if any) of that country can be denounced as "bourgeois". No wonder those North Americans who believe in a reality like this have trouble with the testimony of the new work writing concerning their own society.

A second negative response to the contemporary industrial poems stems from literary scholars and teachers. As considered above in "The Limits of Realism", I believe the attitude of these people to the new work literature arises partly from an alienated perception which equates the obscure in art with quality. Academics and teachers claim it is their vocation to investigate, criticize and pass on to the next generation the productions of the fine arts. Yet the majority of Canadians regard the arts with indifference. This indifference is the mirror image of the attitude with which the arts greet the central life experience of the bulk of the population—daily work. And this same indifference is also directed by the academy toward most of the new artistic productions which seek to express the conditions of daily work in our society.

A second reason for this attitude of scholars and teachers to the new writing seems to be that though their training has equipped them to study and pass judgment on a list of approved literary artifacts, they feel inadequate to apply their expertise to an assessment of other literary productions. Yet whether due to adoption of an alienated perception or due to a lack of confidence in their professional training, the academics' usual reaction to the new industrial literature has an immediate negative effect on this writing. Developing authors who because of their personal experiences have the potential to portray the contemporary working life in many cases decline to do so. The attitude of the academy toward the subject of work suggests to these new artists that this is not a fit concern of art. So they learn to leave behind their knowledge of the working life and to adopt subject matter regarded as more worthy of serious artistic consideration. The academy not only deprives the work writing movement of many potential contributors enrolled in colleges or universities. Also often persuaded to turn to other topics are those who come in contact with and are convinced by teachers, established authors, critics and others who have accepted the prevailing academic opinions as to what constitutes significant art.

It may be that the roots of the academy's disinterest in daily work as a central and important matter lie in the history of university studies. Academic inquiry and discussion, especially in the humanities, goes back to an ecclesiastical tradition which looked to sources other than the secular world as the origins of wisdom. Indeed, the further a concern was from everyday experience, the more it seemed to speak of the divine font of knowlege.

When we examine what the academy today does teach about literature, however, its disinclination to consider seriously the new industrial writing seems somewhat absurd. One of the justifications for the study and teaching of literature is that imaginative writing supposedly contains insight into human existence useful to its readers. But since our literature to date almost entirely omits an examination of the governing activity of daily life for most of us, how useful can this literature's insights really be?

Individual literary scholars may have a personal background which includes familiarity with working milieus other than the academy. But overall, most scholars attempt to weigh the artistic strengths and weaknesses of literary works according to a system of values which incorporates rather less than the whole human experience. And what are the tools with which an academic critic carries out his or her tasks? One currently-voguish approach to literature is mythic criticism. This technique seeks in contemporary and previous imaginative writing patterns of human behavior which either correspond to certain ancient tales involving the supernatural, or that seem to the critic to illuminate human existence as ably as these ancient tales do.

Yet ancient myths can be viewed as attempts by early civilizations to comprehend and explain their world. As such, they and their modern literary equivalents are an outdated technology; they are a means of depicting the human condition in exaggerated terms which has been bypassed in favor of more effective and more accurate methods. A knowledge of outdated technologies may be useful to a historian. But I believe to teach these technologies to literature classes as if they were an adequate approach for examining and understanding the modern era is the equivalent of continuing to instruct psychology students in phrenology.

Of course, scholars whose main critical training is in classical and literary myth will continue to find myths everywhere. They have no other technique readily available to them to scrutinize or discuss literature. And the kind of imaginative writing they will encourage (and create themselves, if they are also writers) is precisely that literature which incorporates and is capable of being discussed in terms of myth.

Yet mythic criticism, like any critical school based on material remote from most people's daily experiences, inevitably produces a jargon unfamiliar to ordinary citizens. Thus, if someone wishes to become a professional literary scholar, he or she must be taught a new language as well as the approved ways of considering literature. In practice, this process of training literary academics incorporates many of the same techniques used in basic training of army inductees: an instilling of the habit of obedience in the trainee by the assignment of meaningless and time-consuming tasks; forced acceptance by the trainee of the world view of the trainer through a system of rewards and punishments; and the removal of the trainee from the usual civilian frames of reference, including common sense.

The results of an educational process so distanced from the concerns of everyday life are poor. The trivial nature of much literary research is already a byword among people with any sort of perspective on the literary scholar's occupation. The failure of university English classes to generate enthusiasm for either the classics of our literature or for contemporary imaginative writing is evidenced in the reading habits of a majority of the population—both those who attended these classes themselves and those who were instructed in school by those who attended these classes. The lack of a command of English spelling, grammar and composition on the part of university graduates is an old complaint, but at best the situation is not improving.

In addition, the current training and practice of most literary scholars ensures that contemporary criticism, like contemporary literature, will not develop into an opportunity for accurate critical reflection on society but remains an elaborate game with esoteric rules. For example, thousands of people undertake the task of constructing metaphors to "explain" literary artifacts, metaphors which often can be applied to the literature under consideration only via a distortion or abridgement of what the authors say. Meanwhile, class after class of students are taught to attempt the same exercise. These students are mainly bored or flabbergasted by this procedure, but here and there a student will resolve to devote himself or herself to mastering this "professional" behavior. And so the pattern is reproduced again. What could be a chance for students to acquire skills necessary for an intelligent and creative assessment of what words can do—not just in literature but also in advertising, politics, and other experiences of everyday existence—instead becomes a means by which students learn that a work of literature is a puzzle which is difficult and probably pointless to try to solve.

Lorraine and Fredy Perlman are convinced that the further a person in our society is located from productive work the more aberrant their behavior becomes. The Perlmans find this applies particularly to academics engaged in study which benefits the war industries.

> Extremely articulate, highly educated and very cultured individuals engage increasingly in activities which, if performed by a working man, would lead to his commitment to a mental hospital for life, with universal approval. It is hard to find peasants or workers who spend years devising methods to derail trains, who develop plastics that will burn while sticking to the skin of a human being, who concoct poisons for a town's water supply, who design concentration camps for people they consider threats to their Country's security, who devote their lives to growing germs which can annihilate a year's harvest.... These people are not considered deranged; each is considered an expert in a field.... They are among the best lodged, best fed and best entertained members of modern society.

I feel parallels to this assessment of war researchers can be made in evaluating the actions of many literary scholars. Certainly no one dies as a result of their academic work. But they nevertheless are well rewarded for ignoring major areas of human experience while they claim they help people understand the world, for discouraging an interest in reading while they claim they teach an appreciation of imaginative writing, for sending thousands of students as well as themselves up the blind alleys of silly research while they claim they instruct people in critical thinking, and for thus wasting students' time, energy and opportunities to study and write.

So these failures of literary academics do considerable harm to other people. And practitioners of other occupations, who might have benefited from meaningful exposure to the (however limited) viewpoints of our literature, are denied by the shortcomings of most literary teachers this opportunity to expand their mental horizons and their abilities. As an engineering professor, writing in the University of Toronto *Bulletin* (Sept. 22, 1980), said:

> Another worrisome situation arises in the teaching of English to engineering students. Are courses in science fiction which are taken by so many engineering undergraduates helpful to them either culturally or in becoming better engineers?...If (C.P.) Snow was right, that it is impossible for literary intellectuals to understand the scientific revolution, then the engineering revolution is even more obscure to them, and we can look for little help in that direction.
>
> How are we to solve this dilemma? Communication in the English language, economics, social impact of technology, and philosophy, ethics...are all essential to the calling of the engineer, yet apparently are beyond the capability of most professors in humanities and social sciences. It appears now that these will be taught primarily by engineering professors who have dual or multiple training and interests or capabilities. Where there are identifiable professors in

> humanities and social sciences who are genuinely interested and do not regard the teaching of engineering undergraduates as an unproductive and barely tolerable burden, they would be welcome and useful in team teaching, pairing these literary intellectuals with our engineering intellectuals.... Perhaps this process...might be furthered by recognition of its goals: to graduate engineers who, when they eventually undertake the design of engineering works, will take into full account not only their technical and economic feasibility but their social feasibility, engineers whose philosophy and ethics, whose professionalism, will lead them to achieve *moral* designs, to be engineers who serve society.

The study of literature *could* effect all that it now claims to do, I believe, if it accepted as its basis the same engagement with the actual conditions of daily life that the new industrial writing does. Literary scholarship then would consist of a particular era assessing the imaginative writing of its own time and of earlier periods, but in the light of social history, geography, economics and numerous other disciplines, not excluding the histories to date of literature and criticism. This would require that literary scholars be generalists, men and women with an informed overview of human achievements in many spheres. Just as scientists are now expected to have a mastery of English language rules and composition, so the new literary scholars would be expected to have a thorough comprehension and some practice of modern science and many other areas of human knowledge, in order to think about and comment intelligently on literature's relationship to our daily lives. Foremost in what the new scholar would have to be aware of, then, would be the everyday working life in our society. It is here that all human progress is created. And this is where the real state of that progress, of human emancipation, can be measured.

At present, there is enormous pressure on all human beings, academics no less than imaginative writers, *not* to consider the conditions of daily work and its consequences. One cause of this is the nature of our jobs. As Marx argues in his *Economic and Philosophic Manuscripts of 1844* (cited here from Selsam and Martel, eds., *Reader in Marxist Philosophy* [New York: International, 1964]), when an employee in his or her work

> does not affirm himself but denies himself, does not feel content but unhappy, does not develop freely his physical and mental energy but mortifies his body and ruins his mind

then that person

> only feels himself outside his work, and in his work feels outside himself. He is at home when he is not working, and when he is working he is not at home.

The situation described by Marx is well understood by the originators of the mass consumption artifacts which now surround us. These people use against us how our work makes us feel, by selling us a range of products and services to be consumed after work which supposedly restores our manhood or femininity. As Marx says:

> ...man (the worker) no longer feels himself to be freely active in any but his animal functions—eating, drinking, procreating, or at most in his dwelling and in dressing-up, etc.; and in his human functions he no longer feels himself to be

> anything but an animal. What is animal becomes human and what is human becomes animal.
>
> Certainly eating, drinking, procreating, etc., are also genuinely human functions. But in the abstraction which separates them from the sphere of all other human activity and turns them into sole and ultimate ends, they are animal.

No wonder our inclination is to think and write most about those portions of our existence during which we consider ourselves to be most fully and freely alive. Not that life at the jobs is uniformly bleak. There can be satisfaction at working with friends, or even with familiar personalities. There can be feelings of accomplishment as we master new techniques or tools, or we solve various problems which appear during the shift. And we might feel pride at being a member of a particular trade, and so on. But the working conditions that won't let us perform to the best of our ability, or the sense of waiting impatiently for quitting time or Friday, of coming alive at the instant of punching out for the day or leaving the office, all tell us the job is dead time for us, too.

Though these working conditions strongly affect our lives, we are not automatons, however. The present schemes for organizing production are human constructs, and we as human beings can improve or discard them. As we examine what happens at the jobs, we can see how to change work for the better. And literature and criticism could be of assistance in this. One of the slogans of the 1968 Paris May was "Vivre sans temps mort"—live without dead time. The challenge that this ideal proposes is to collectively bring as much human thought and experience together as we can, in order to take back these hours that we work for others, to make them or their equivalents economically, physically, mentally our own.

The urge toward narrow specialization, which I suggest above be abandoned by literary academics, is also partly a consequence of the job, of the trend toward a high degree of division of labor in modern industry. But again: the present forms of production were established by people, and people can devise more satisfying methods of creating goods and services. The existing factory and wage systems do not mark the limits of human ingenuity or ability. And by refusing to be narrowly specialized, we commit an act of resistance against the way our industrial society defines people.

The new industrial authors have already begun to demolish some of society's categories. At present, workers are supposed to work and writers write. If a "writer" is employed at a job, he or she is supposed to consider himself or herself not "really" a worker. This is identical to the way, as mentioned above in "Regional Culture, National Culture, Industrial Culture", those around the writer on the job have learned to consider themselves really farmers, evangelical Christians, hang glider pilots, and so on. The new work poets say: "No. I work and I write. *Both* are part of my life."

This declaration also once more counters the Romantic image of the artist as someone out of control, unable to hold a job, irresponsible, mad. This image, fostered as well by the mass consumption media, permits the rest of us to seldom consider being creative in this way ourselves. We're supposed to conclude that since an artist is nuts, and we're not crazy, we could never be a true artist. Also, should art ever include a critique of society, the potential audience has already been predisposed to dismiss that critique on the grounds that art is the work of fools or weirdos anyway. But the new work writers reject this definition of an author, and so insist on the right of each person to have access to creativity in the arts as in every aspect of existence throughout the day.

The English art critic John Berger has written (in *A Seventh Man* [Harmondsworth: Penguin, 1975]) about the consequences to a person of accepting the definitions this society usually applies to people. Berger in the following quote is talking specifically about the superior attitude of European employees toward migrants brought in from other countries to make up a labor shortage in certain industries. This attitude of superiority is part of the set of values that allows us at the same time to view ourselves as inferior to others, Berger says. His idea can be applied to the concept that art is something other people do—whether we consider artists crazy, or superior to ourselves:

> The principle of natural inequality rests upon judging men and women according to their abilities. It is obvious that ability varies, and that abilities are unequally distributed.... What determines a person's position in the social hierarchy is the sum of his abilities as required in that particular social and economic system. He is no longer seen as another man, as the unique centre of his own experience: he is seen as the mere conglomerate of certain capacities and needs. He is seen, in other words, as a complex of functions within a social system. And he can never be seen as more than that unless the notion of equality between men is reintroduced.
>
> Equality has nothing to do with capacity or function: it is the recognition of being.... Only in relation to what men are in their entirety can a social system be judged just or unjust: otherwise it can be merely assessed as relatively efficient or inefficient. The principle of equality is the revolutionary principle, not only because it challenges hierarchies, but because it asserts that all men are equally whole. And the converse is just as true: to accept inequality as natural is to become fragmented, is to see oneself as no more than the sum of a set of capacities and needs....

> When the indigenous worker accepts inequality as the principle to sustain his own self-esteem, he reinforces and completes the fragmentation which society is already imposing upon him.
>
> That this will continue to happen is the calculation of the ruling class.

By refusing to accept the categories that define working people as incapable of imaginative writing, the new industrial authors raise the possibility of a different life: one where the work we do does not have to limit us, define us as superior to some and inferior to others, or make us invisible during that part of the day which governs the quality of the rest of our lives. To suggest this possibility is part of the contribution the industrial writers make toward the rebuilding of the world a better way.

And the new work literature shows that this rebuilding must be an inside job, with those of us who are employed acting ourselves to improve our daily existence. Otherwise, a reorganization of society will amount to nothing more than the imposition of new social hierarchies while factory, shop and office life continues unaltered (or is made worse).

Meanwhile, although the authoritarian left cannot accept the implications of the new industrial literature, and although the academy cannot recognize contemporary work as a serious subject for art, these two groups are reflections of the current social structure rather than responsible for it. Their opposition to the new writing is not likely to lessen while the present system of production exists. But the appearance of the new industrial literature seems to me symptomatic of some important changes happening in the North American work force. And whatever the causes, and whatever occurs as the consequences of the changes become evident, I am convinced these changes in the long run will prove to be as beneficial to our society, to daily life, as they already have begun to be to literature.

Selected Bibliography (1973-1982)

Anthologies

Carson, Robert, ed. *The Waterfront Writers* (San Francisco: Harper & Row, 1979). Poetry and fiction on San Francisco longshore work.

Gom, Leona, ed. *Event* magazine, work issue, vol. 11 no. 1 Spring 1982 (Surrey B.C.: Kwantlen College, 1982). Fiction and poetry by U.S. and Canadian writers about different jobs.

O'Rourke, William, ed. *On the Job* (New York: Random House, 1977). Short stories and excerpts from novels by U.S. writers about various jobs.

Senna (Barbara Banfield), Mona Bachmann, Emily Martha Sparrowhawk Brandon, eds. *Women Working* (Seattle: Women Working, 1980). Poetry by U.S. women writers about different jobs.

Waterfront Writers and Artists, eds. *Waterfront Writers and Artists* (San Francisco: Waterfront Writers and Artists 1980). Poetry by U.S. and Canadian writers about maritime jobs.

Wayman, Tom, ed. *Going For Coffee* (Madeira Park, B.C.: Harbour Publishing, 1981). Poetry by U.S. and Canadian writers about a range of jobs.

Individual Authors—books entirely or mainly about working

Antler. *Factory* (San Francisco: City Lights, 1980). Long poem from Milwaukee can factory.

Beaver, David. *No Free Rides* (Vancouver, B.C.: MacLeod & Stewart, 1980). Poems on taxi driving in Vancouver.

Brill, Ernie. *I Looked Over Jordan and Other Stories* (Boston: South End Press, 1980). Short stories about U.S. hospital work.

Christensen, Peter. *Rig Talk* (Saskatoon: Thistledown, 1981). Poems about Alberta oilfield employment.

Conn, David. *Harbour Light* (Fredericton, N.B.: Fiddlehead, 1976). Poems on Vancouver shipyard work.

———. *Ticket Stubs for the Bullgang* (Vancouver, B.C.: Caitlin Press, 1980). Poems on Vancouver shipyard work.

Cote, Oliver. *Going Down* (San Pedro, CA: Singlejack Books 1979). Novel about Detroit welfare casework.

Daniels, Jim. *Factory Poems* (Alma, MI: Jack in the Box Press, 1979). Poems about Ford auto assembly.

———. *On the Line* (Bellingham, WA: Signpost Press, 1981). Poems about Ford auto assembly.

Day, David. *The Cowichan* (Madeira Park, B.C.: Harbour Publishing, 1976). Poems on B.C. coast logging.

Fennario, David. *On the Job* (Vancouver, B.C.: Talonbooks, 1976). Play about Montreal garment factory work.

Fried, Emanuel. *The Dodo Bird* (Buffalo, NY: Labor Arts, 1975). Play about western New York factory employees.

———. *Drop Hammer* (Cambridge, MA: West End Press/Labor Arts, 1977). Play about unions in Buffalo, New York, heavy industry.

Glaberman, Martin. *The Grievance* (San Pedro, CA: Singlejack Books, 1980). Poems about Detroit auto production jobs.

Hauser, Gwen. *The Ordinary Invisible Woman* (Fredericton, N.B.: Fiddlehead, 1978). Poems on various Toronto factory jobs.

Jewinski, Hans. *Poet Cop* (Markham, Ont.: Pocket Books, 1975). Poems by a Toronto police constable.

Lee, David. *The Porcine Legacy* (Port Townsend, WA: Copper Canyon Press, 1978). Poems about pig farming.

McLean, Jim. *The Secret Life of Railroaders* (Moose Jaw, Sask.: Coteau Books, 1982). Poems by a railway carman.

Marty, Sid. *Headwaters* (Toronto: McClelland & Stewart, 1973). Poems on employment as a national park warden.

Muska, Nick. *Elm (Warehouse Poems 1974-1977)* (Toledo, OH: Toledo Poets Center Press, 1979). Poems on warehouse work.

Potrebenko, Helen. *Taxi* ! (Vancouver, B.C.: New Star, 1975). Novel on taxi driving in Vancouver.

Roberts, Kevin. *Deep Line* (Madeira Park, B.C.: Harbour Publishing, 1978). Poems about B.C. coast commercial fishing.

Scott, Herbert. *Groceries* (Pittsburgh: University of Pittsburgh Press, 1976). Poems on supermarket employment.

Skapski, John. *Green Water Blues* (Madeira Park, B.C.: Harbour Publishing, 1978). Poems about B.C. coast commercial fishing.

Trower, Peter. *Bush Poems* (Madeira Park, B.C.: Harbour Publishing, 1978). Poems about B.C. coast logging.

Warrior, M.C. *Quitting Time* (Vancouver, B.C.: MacLeod Books, 1978). Poems about B.C. coast logging.

White, Howard. *The Men There Were Then* (Vancouver, B.C.: Arsenal Pulp Press, 1982). Poems on a range of jobs from driving cat to shucking oysters.

Zimpel, Lloyd. *Foundry Foreman, Foundryman* (San Pedro, CA: Singlejack Books, 1980). Short stories about U.S. foundry labor.

Individual Authors—books which include some work material

Green, Jim. *North Book* (Burnaby, B.C.: Blackfish Press, 1975). Poems about Arctic outdoor work.

Hauser, Gwen. *Hands Get Lonely Sometimes* (Vancouver, B.C.: blewointment press, 1977). Poems on various Toronto factory jobs.

Lane, Patrick. *Poems New and Selected* (Toronto: Oxford, 1978). Poems about different B.C. Interior mill and outdoor jobs.

Marty, Sid. *Nobody Danced With Miss Rodeo* (Toronto: McClelland & Stewart, 1981). Poems on employment as a national park warden.

Wayman, Tom. *Money And Rain* (Toronto: Macmillan of Canada, 1975). Poems on Vancouver motor truck assembly.